BOYS' MAKE-AT-HOME THINGS

LECTOR HOUSE PUBLIC DOMAIN WORKS

BOYS' MAKE-AT-HOME THINGS

CAROLYN SHERWIN BAILEY, MARIAN ELIZABETH BAILEY

ISBN: 978-93-93693-91-4

Published: 1912

LECTOR HOUSE LLP
E-MAIL: lectorpublishing@gmail.com

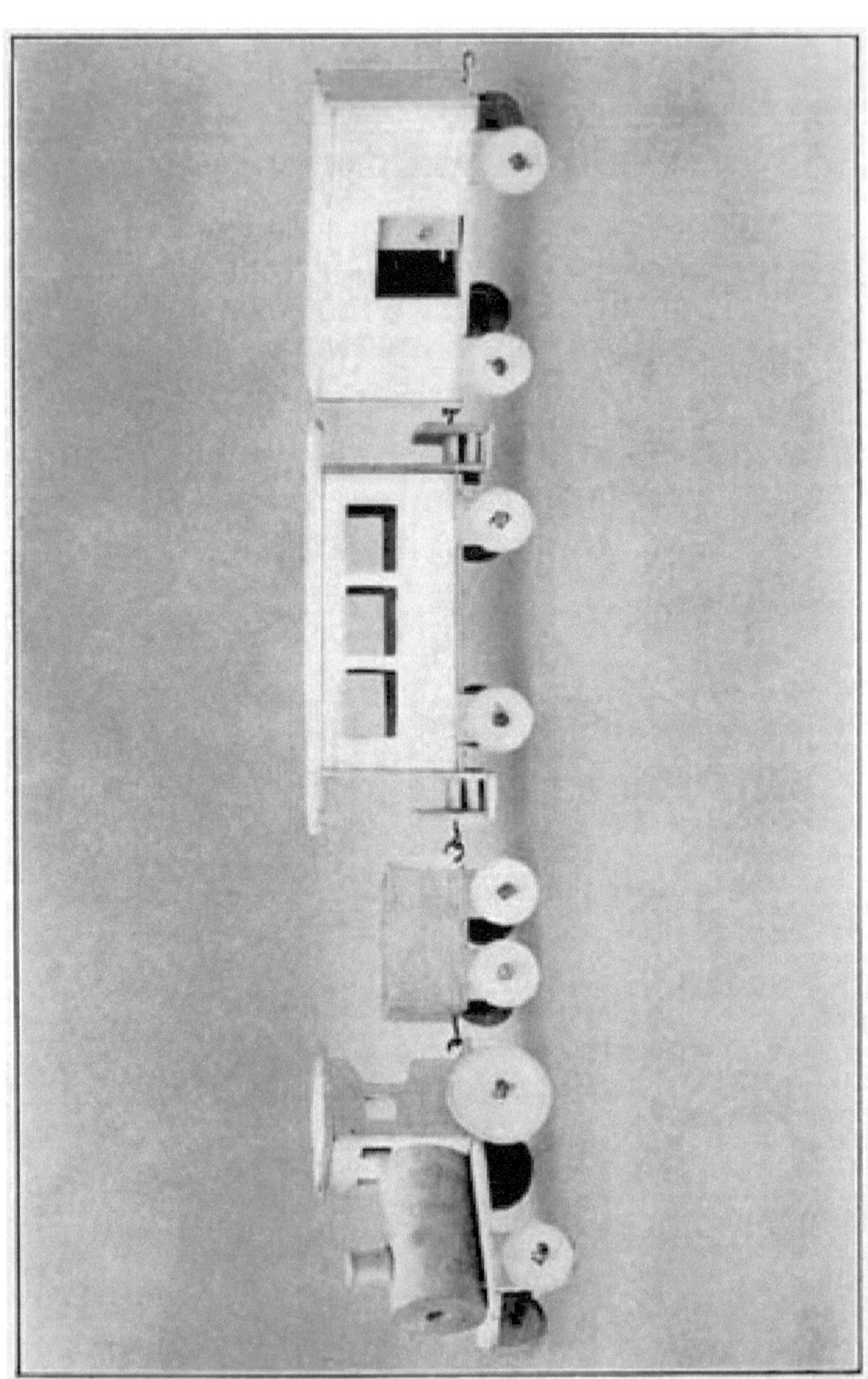

Whittled Toy Train.

BOYS' MAKE-AT-HOME THINGS

BY

CAROLYN SHERWIN BAILEY
AND
MARIAN ELIZABETH BAILEY

WITH NUMEROUS ILLUSTRATIONS AND DIAGRAMS

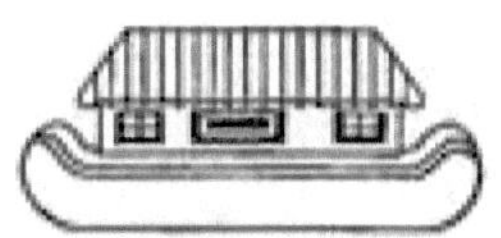

1912

PREFACE

Make-At-Home-Things for Boys aims to keep boys busy and entertained. It furnishes them with simple directions for making toys and useful articles, all of which are carefully pictured. The aim of the book, is to give boys an idea of the craft possibilities which lie in the crudest materials, often the waste material of the home and in this way to develop real artistic ability.

CONTENTS

LIST OF ILLUSTRATIONS

BOYS' MAKE-AT-HOME THINGS

THE MAKING OF TOOLS
NECESSARY FOR WHITTLING

THE tools which one will need for whittling—the kind of whittling that makes something besides splinters—are very simple and few in number. Any boy's pocket will furnish a jack-knife, and it is pretty sure to be a sharp one.

With a knife, a pencil, and some pieces of wood, all the other tools may be made. Basswood is the easiest wood to handle because it is soft, and very close grained. If basswood can not be had, pine is the next best wood, and an old egg crate, which any grocer will be glad to get rid of, will furnish you with enough whittling material for a long time.

The scale for measuring (Fig. 3) should be made first, as it is the tool most necessary in laying out the other tools. One of the thin strips from the side of the egg crate may be used for this. The outline of the scale must be drawn on the wood with a hard pencil. A "6 H" is the best. The "H" means "hard," and the number of H's shows the degree of hardness. The pencil should be sharpened on both ends—one end rubbed to a fine point on sandpaper, and the other end to a chisel point. The sharp point is to mark, accurately, the points to which lines are to be drawn, and the chisel point is to draw the lines with. After the outline is drawn it may be cut.

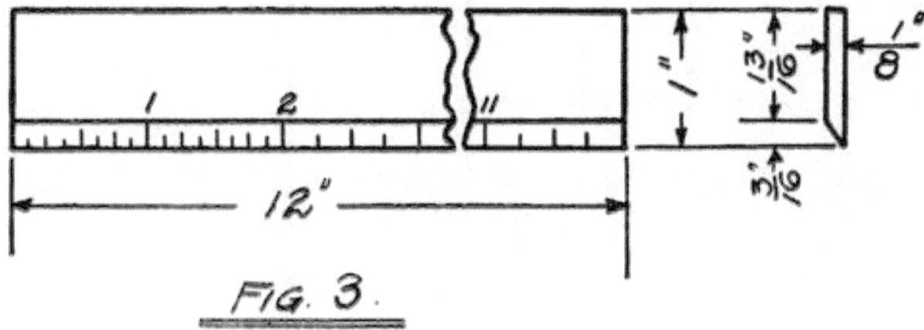

FIG. 3.

First take off a splinter or two to determine the direction of the grain, because one long cut against the grain might spoil your work. When this is determined, you should cut down *almost* to the outline, using a long, free stroke from the shoulder for the cutting in the direction of the grain. For the cross-grained cutting at the ends, the knife is held in the four fingers, with the thumb steadying the near side of the wood, and the cut is made toward the thumb. Only a very short cut may be made at a time, and then a bit of wood is clipped away so that the next cut may be made. This cutting, also, should be done near, but not on, the line. After the model is roughly cut out, it should be worked down very carefully to the lines, the beveled edge cut, and then sandpapered smooth all over. The sandpaper must be put over a small block of wood, and held very flat. Otherwise it will spoil a straight surface. Then the graduations are to be put on. If nothing better is at hand, the spacing may be done with mother's tape measure. Lay off the spaces with the pointed end of the pencil, and then draw the lines which show the spacing, making those which show the sixteenths, $\frac{1}{16}$" long; the eighths, $\frac{1}{8}$" long; the quarters, $\frac{3}{16}$" long; the halves, $\frac{5}{16}$", or the full width of the bevel. This must be done with a pencil, for ink would run into the wood and spread. The inch dimensions should be marked 1, 2, 3, etc., and a light coat of shellac or varnish will add much to the durability of the scale. The back edge of the scale may be used as a straight edge, and to lay the pencil against for drawing lines, but it should be remembered that the scale itself—that is, the graduated side—must never be used for this. If it were, the graduations would soon be spoiled.

The tool which is most necessary next to the scale is the square (Fig. 4), and this should also be made with great accuracy. It is used to test two adjoining edges, to see if they are square with each other. In making anything of wood, one of the largest surfaces is generally made perfectly true, and marked with a little cross (x), designating it as the "face." One of the adjoining edges—not a cross-grained one—is also made true and square with the first surface, and marked with a second cross, as the "working edge." Then all the other measuring and squaring is done from these two surfaces.

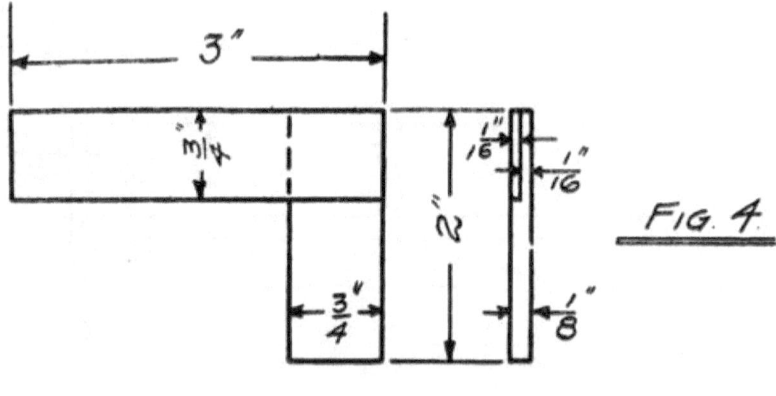

FIG. 4.

The piece of wood to be tested should be held in the left hand, on a level with the eye, and the square held in the right hand, with one of the inner edges resting against the wood, and the other projecting over it is moved back and forth. Any unevenness in the wood will readily be seen. The outside edges of the square may also be used for testing the evenness of wide flat surfaces. It is made like the pattern, of two strips of wood, with a fitted joint glued together.

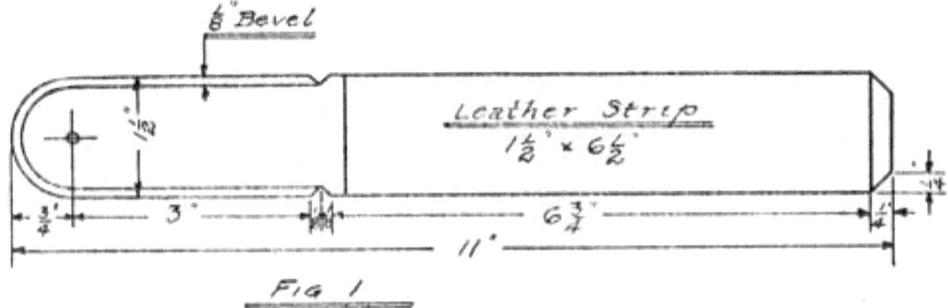

FIG. 1.

The knife strop shown in Fig. 1 is a great help in whittling, because it will keep your knife in good condition. A piece of the heavier wood at the end of the egg crate may be used for this. It is made from a strip measuring 1½" wide by 11" long, and the strip of leather (cut from a discarded razor strop) is glued on. The ⅛" bevel is continued all the way around the handle on both sides to make it fit the hand. The hole in the end is to hang it up by, and may be made with a hammer and nail, or with a bit and brace if you have one.

The pencil sharpener (Fig. 2), is also a very necessary help in whittling and it is very simple to make. A strip of thin wood 1¼"x7" forms the foundation. This is narrowed down at the handle end to ¾". The curves may be marked on the outline, free hand, and in cutting you must be very careful to remember the grain of the wood. The curves at the ends should be cut from each side toward the middle of the end, gradually working into a cross-cut. The curves at the sides must be cut from the wider part toward the handle, using the point of the knife, and working with great care so as not to split the wood. A strip of sandpaper 1"x3" is glued on and the sharpener is complete.

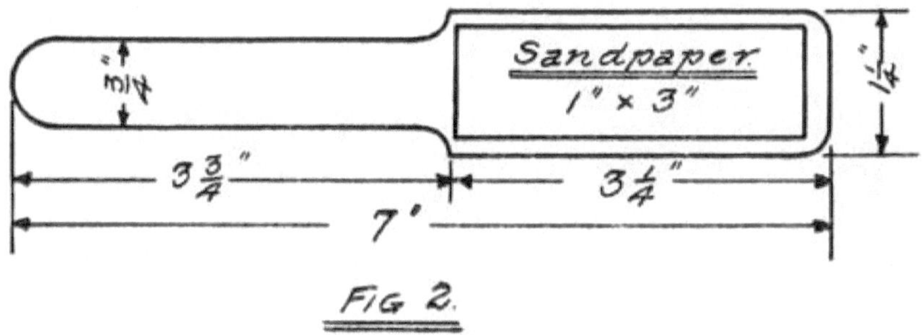

FIG. 2.

With these tools finished a boy is ready to begin some real whittling, and make other models which will be quite as useful, and very much more attractive.

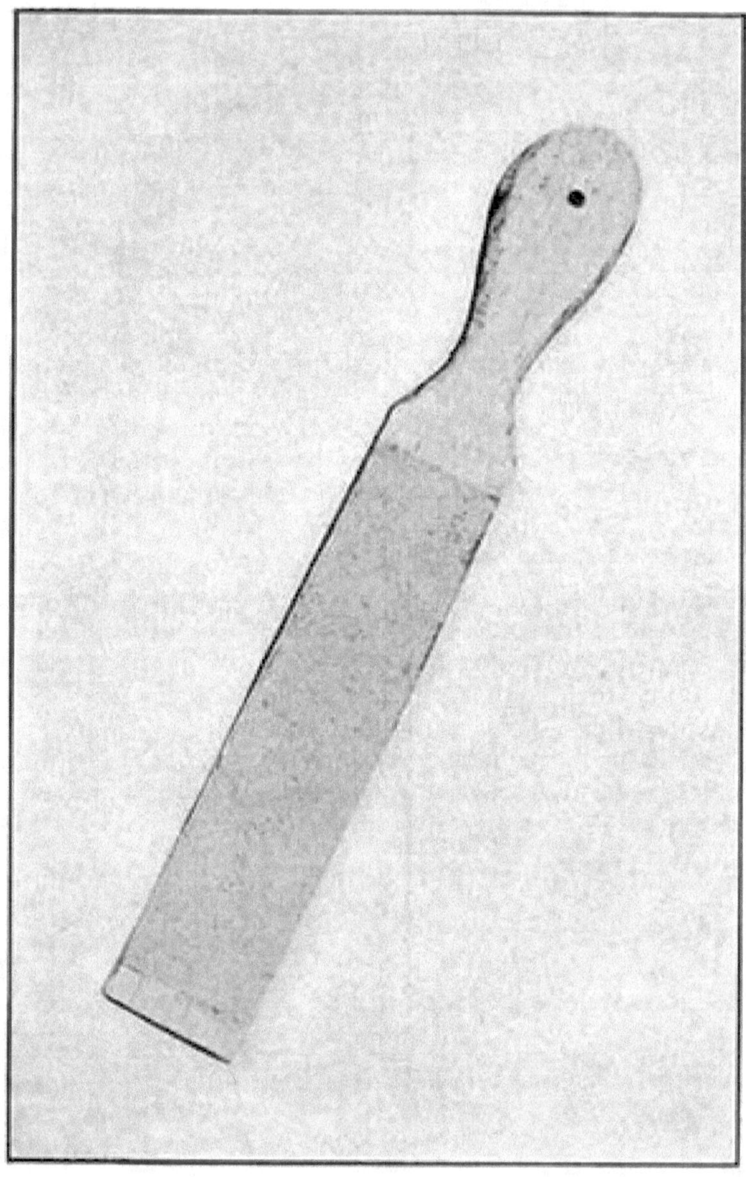

Knife-strop.

HOW TO MAKE A PRACTICAL WORK BENCH

A GOOD practical workbench may be made by any boy who can handle the simplest tools and procure a little suitable lumber.

The lumber should be bought at a lumber yard, in the rough, which will cost a great deal less than finished boards.

It will require 26 ft. of two-by-four pine boards, 12 ft. of two-by-six's, and 23 ft. of one-by-six's. The two-by-four's cost one and three-quarters cents a running foot, the two-by-six's are two and a half cents, and the one-by-six's, one and a half cents. The boards come in regular lengths, from ten feet up to sixteen, or in some cases, up to twenty-four feet long. It will be best to get a twenty-four foot one-by-six board if possible, a twelve foot two-by-six, one twelve foot and one fourteen foot two-by-four. This will make the total cost for boards one dollar and twelve cents.

Aside from the pine boards for the bench itself it will require a piece of oak measuring three by four inches and thirty-four inches long, for the bench vise; a screw and handle for the vise (costing thirty-five cents at any hardware store); a pound of four inch nails; and two square headed iron bolts, one half inch in diameter and four inches long, each fitted with two iron washers and one square nut.

Saw off, first, from the twelve foot two-by-four, four pieces thirty-three inches long. These are the legs of the bench, and they are to stand with their broad four-inch faces toward the ends of the bench. Then cut in each one of these joints like those shown in Fig. 1. The sides in which the joints are cut face toward each other at the ends of the bench and into them is fitted the supporting framework.

For the lower framework cut from the fourteen foot two-by-four two pieces forty-two inches long and four pieces nineteen inches long. Two of the nineteen-inch pieces are to be left as they are, but the other two and the two forty-two inch pieces should have joints cut at the ends like Fig. 2. These joints, as well as the joints in the uprights, are cut with a saw, and the wood is split out with a chisel. Then these four jointed pieces are fitted together and glued or nailed to form a framework nineteen by forty-two inches. The four uprights are then fitted in place and nailed, increasing the width of the ends to twenty-three inches. Then the other two nineteen-inch pieces are fitted into the top of the uprights across each end, and nailed in place. Four braces (Fig. 3) for the ends are made from two sixteen-inch pieces of the one-by-six stock. Each piece is first cut in two, lengthwise, with a rip saw. This makes four pieces twenty inches long by three inches wide. Mark the center joint of each end of each piece. Then measure on both sides, from each end, a distance of one and a half inches. Connect these points with the end points by a line and saw off the corners, leaving on each end a right-angled point. The braces are then nailed in place as shown in Fig. 4.

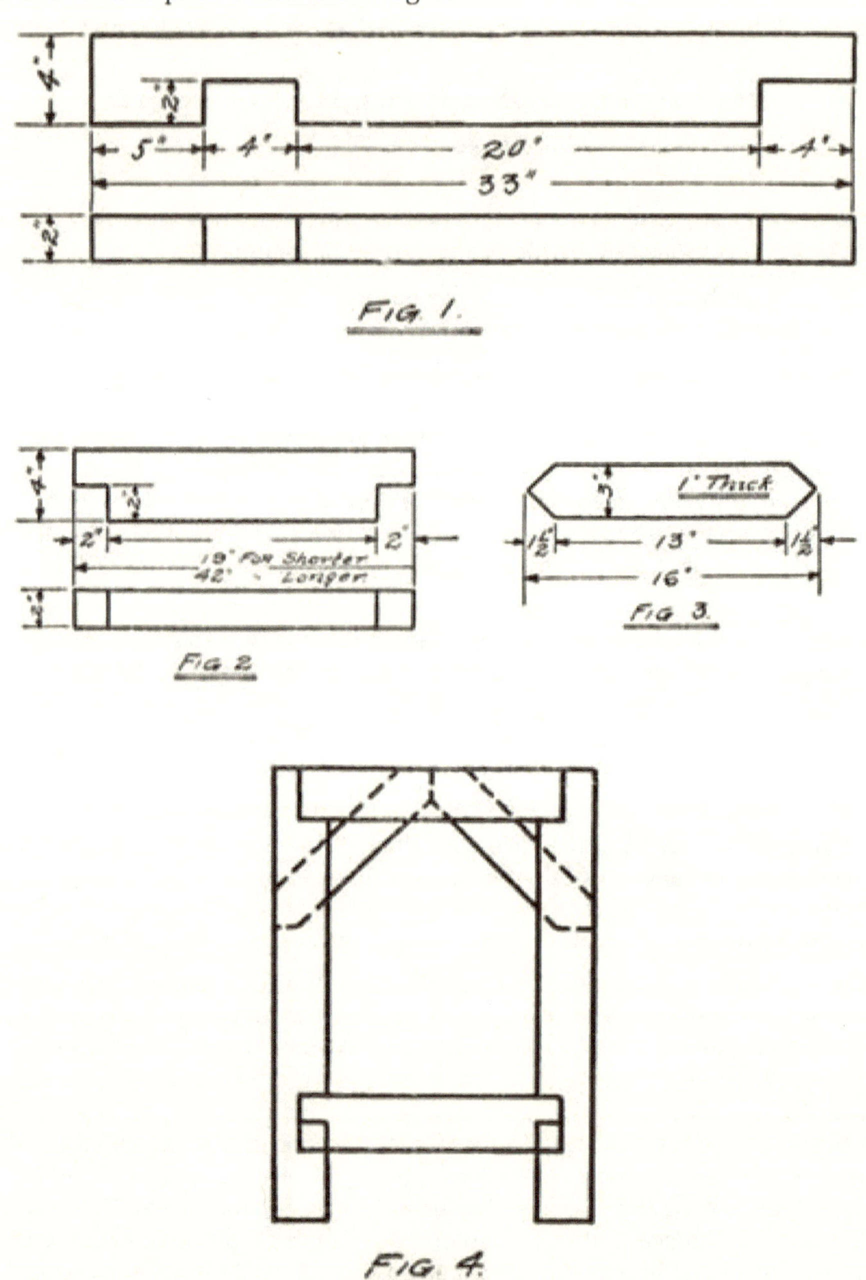

Diagrams of a Practical Work-bench.

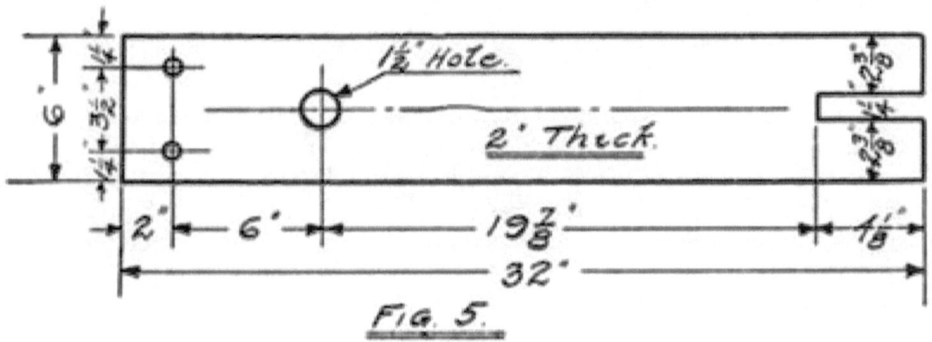

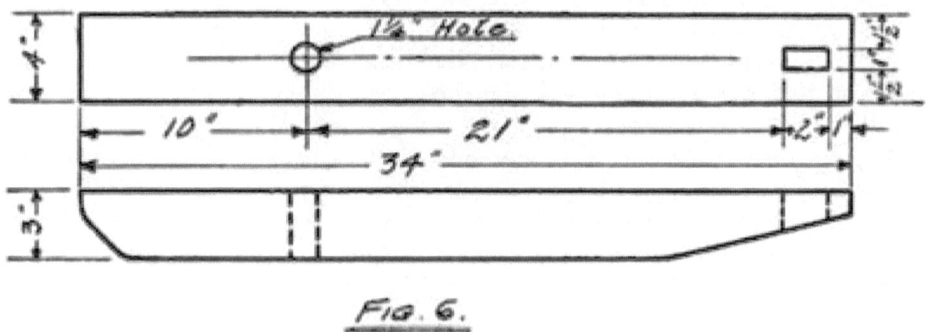

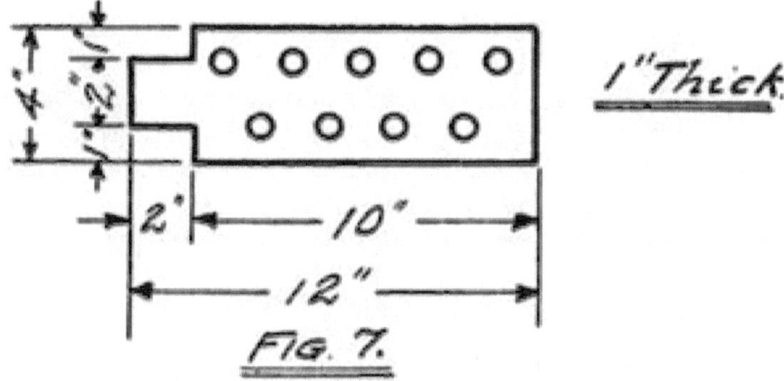

Diagrams of a Practical Work-bench.

This finishes the body part of the bench. Next, cut from the one-by-six board a piece fifty-six inches long. Fit it across the front of the frame, just even, or flush with the top, and projecting seven inches beyond the uprights at either end. Then nail in position.

Cut from the twelve foot two-by-six board two pieces fifty-six inches long. Place one of them across the top of the bench at the extreme front, so that it is flush with the wide surface of the front board. Nail this to the end framework and nail the second piece in position just back of it.

It is necessary for this much of the top to be very heavy, for this is where the heavy strain of the work will come. The remainder of the top is made of two strips of one-by-six wood. In order to make this even with the two front strips which are thicker it is necessary to put pieces underneath it at each end. For these cut a piece of one-by-six board twelve inches long and rip it in two. Place these strips along the end frame, then place the top boards on them and nail all in position. When this is done the whole top of the bench may be made partially smooth, if it is desired, with a jack plane. Then cut one more strip of one-by-six fifty-six inches long and nail across the back of the bench, allowing it to project three inches above the top.

The vise, as it comes from the store, consists of a long, straight, square-headed screw about an inch in diameter, which ends in a round iron plate and a T-shaped pipe. The plate is loose but not removable. Through the T a long wooden handle fits. Beside this there is an elliptical plate holding a threaded pipe which the screw works in. To put it together, first make a piece from the remaining two-by-six like Fig. 5. This piece forms the inner side of the vise and fits *inside* of the front piece of the bench, just touching the under side of the top, and *outside* of the lower framework. Its edge should be four inches in from the front leg of the bench. Corresponding holes are made with a bit and brace in the front piece of the bench and counter-sunk a half inch. The two pieces are then bolted together, the heads of the bolts and the iron washer fitting down in the counter-sink, and the other washer being placed under the nut on the other side. The receptacle for the vise screw is fastened in position through the back of Fig. 5.

Next, the piece of oak is prepared for the vise jaw. It is slanted off at the ends like Fig. 6, the outer edges rounded, a hole somewhat larger than the vise screw cut through as shown, and a joint cut through with chisel and hammer near the bottom. Into this joint fit Fig. 7, a piece of wood one by four inches and twelve inches long, which is intended to keep the jaws of the vise approximately even. It fits into the oak with a drive fit and has holes zigzagged or "staggered" across it into which a round peg three inches fits. By placing this peg in different holes the bottom opening of the vise may be adjusted to correspond with the desired top opening.

The long screw of the vise is slipped through the hole made for it, and the plate is screwed in place.

This completes a bench which will prove a great help to the boy workman, and which takes scarcely more time in making than it has in describing.

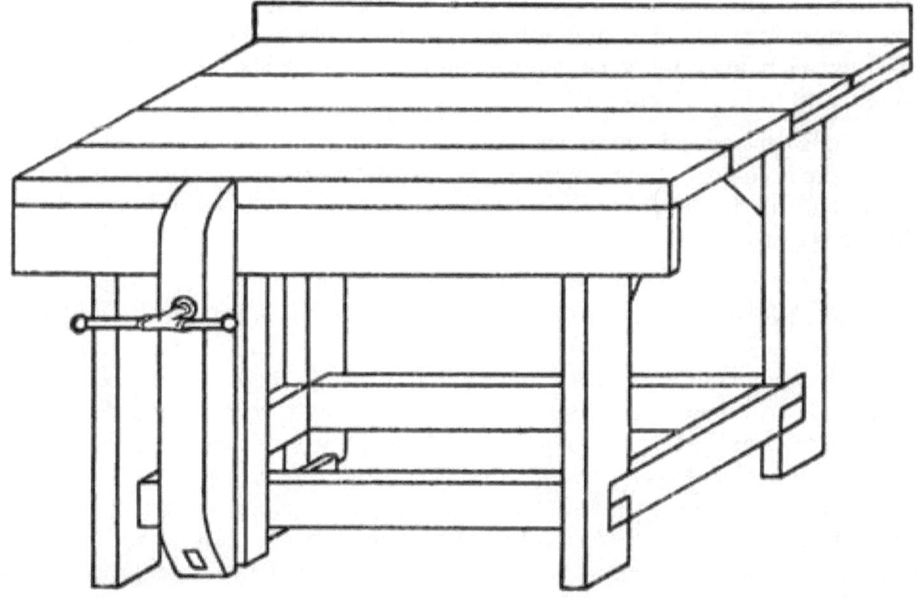

Work Bench Complete.

WORK BENCH ACCESSORIES

WHEN you have made yourself this fine, big workbench you will find out very soon that there are a number of workbench accessories which will make it much more convenient and desirable.

The first thing that will be missed is a tool rack. With tools scattered all over the bench it is difficult to do good work. It means a waste of time and sometimes a waste of temper, while, if the tools are hanging right before one's eyes in an orderly row, each one may be taken as it is needed, and replaced again when one is through, and the work will go on smoothly.

A single pine board six inches wide, one inch thick and sixteen feet long will make all the accessories one can want. It is better to procure a finished board from the planing mill. It will cost three or four cents a running foot—a total cost at the most of sixty-four cents.

For the tool rack cut from the board two fifty-six-inch lengths. Cut one of these in two lengthwise with a rip saw and plane the sawed edge smooth and square with the face or wide, flat side of the board. With a pencil and scale mark the positions on the centers of the holes shown in Fig. 1. Then when the centers have been determined, drill them according to the sizes indicated, with a bit and brace. The first three holes at the left are to hold bits; the next two, chisel and gouge, and the others are for screw-drivers. These latter four, after the holes are drilled, are made open clear to the edge of the rack by sawing out a section from the front. This makes it possible to take the tools out without lifting them entirely out of the rack. From the right-hand end mark off a distance of twelve inches. Then, from the end to this line, cut two grooves as shown in the drawing. The forward one is rounded out with a gouge to hold a pencil while the back one is square and flat, cut with a chisel, to hold either a twelve-inch scale or a folded two-foot rule. In the front edge of this piece, about six inches from the right-hand end is driven a nail to hold the claw hammer.

The fifty-six-inch length which was not ripped in two is fitted at right angles to the back of this rack, lapping over the edge and flush with the top. It is nailed in position and two supporting brackets like Fig. 2 are fitted under each end of the rack for strength. When this is all fastened together, the whole rack is set up on top of the back pieces of the workbench and held in place by two cleats, three inches by eight which are screwed to both the back piece of the bench and the back piece of the rack.

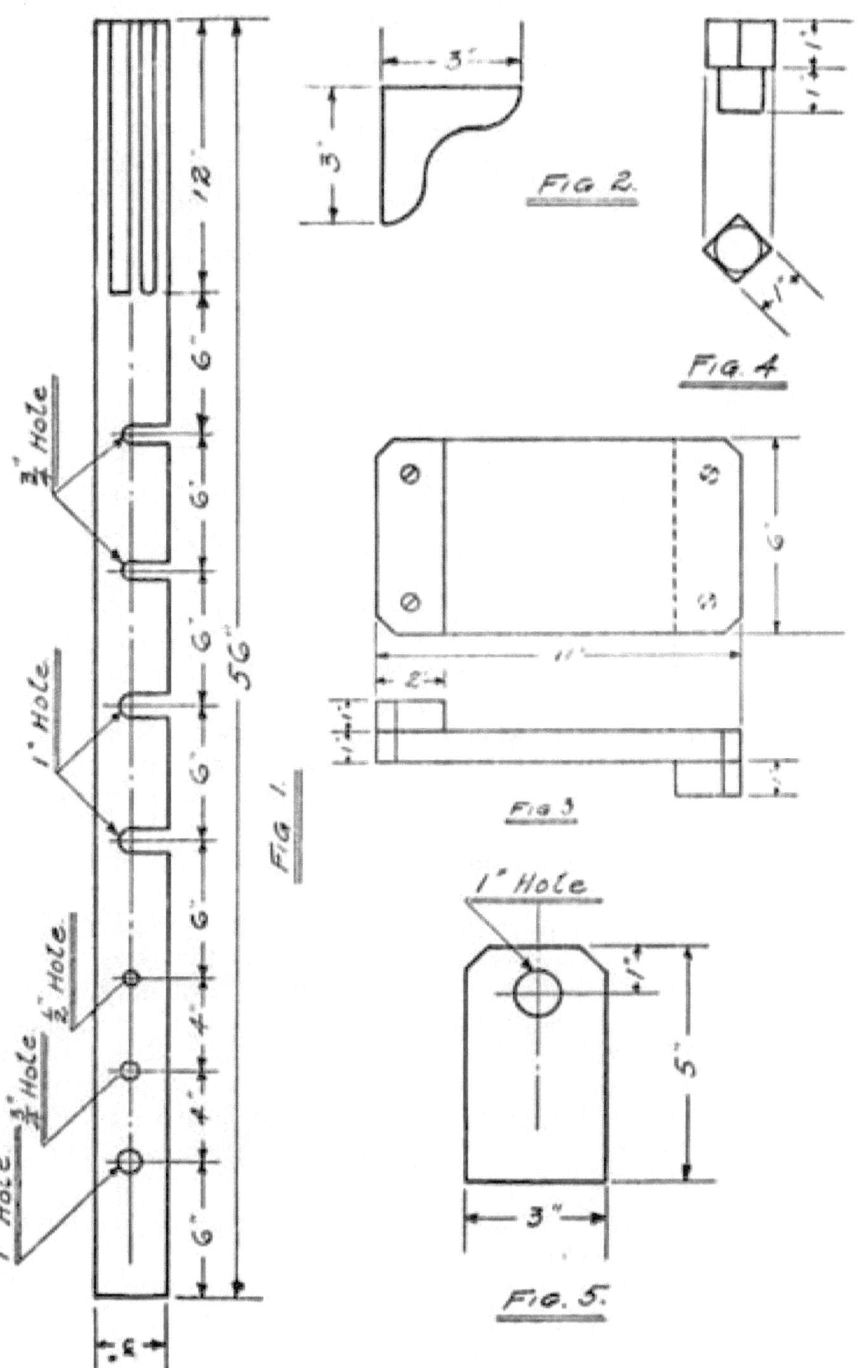

Diagrams of Work-bench Accessories.

Underneath the holes for the bits there should be two nails to hold the brace. The jack plane, block plane, and spoke shave may stand on the bench underneath the rack, and screws or nails at the end of the bench will hold rip saw, cross-cut saw, and dust brush.

Next in usefulness is the bench block shown in Fig. 3. For this cut one piece of wood six inches by eleven, and two pieces, six inches by two inches. All these pieces must have the grain running in the longest direction. When these are trued up, fit them together as shown, and fasten with one-and-three-quarter-inch wood screws. After completing this the corners are cut off. The block fits over the front edge of the bench near the right-hand end and forms a brace when one wants to hold a piece of wood steady for sawing.

Next comes the bench stop, Fig. 4. When one is planing a wide, flat board the vise is useless. So holes are drilled in pairs in the top of the bench itself, and these bench stops are slipped in to form a buffer. A little piece of wood one by one by two is used, the grain of course running the long way. For half of the distance the stop remains square, while the other inch is rounded with a chisel to fit into the hole, which should be slightly more than an inch deep. Two of these stops will be needed.

Every workbench needs a nail box. A good one may be made from two pieces three inches wide by fourteen inches long, which form the sides, two ends three inches by three, and a bottom piece five inches by fourteen. The side pieces are nailed to the end pieces, fitting over them, and the bottom fits over all. This makes the inside measurements three inches by twelve. Of course it is desirable to keep the different sizes of nails separate, so this is divided into as many compartments as are desired by partitions. These can be made from any old piece of wood about a half inch thick. They measure three by three inches and may be spaced however you like, except the one which is shown in Fig. 5. This is to be placed in the middle and forms a handle as well as a partition. Just as convenient, though not quite as necessary, is a miter box. It consists of two side pieces five inches by twelve, and one bottom piece four inches by twelve. The side pieces fit down over the edges of the bottom piece and are nailed fast. There are no ends. When this much is done, take a forty-five degree triangle, and mark across the two top edges one perpendicular line, and one forty-five degree line in each direction, making them so that they do not overlap. Then saw straight down from these lines to the bottom piece. A miter box will prove itself a great convenience in sawing the corners of molding or anything which requires a fitted corner. The piece to be sawed is held firmly in the box and the saw guided through the slots.

When a boy has made the bench and all these accessories, and has some tools, he will be equipped for big practical work.

HOW TO MAKE A TURNING LATHE

MOST boys have a speaking acquaintance with a turning lathe. Some boys know how to use one with good results. But to use one and own it too—that is a joy which few boys experience.

After all, though, a lathe is not such a formidable machine, and if a boy is quick at catching an idea and working it out he can make one for himself.

Most of the material can be procured from some machine shop at practically no cost, and the parts that have to be bought outright will cost very little.

The foundation may be an old sewing-machine stand and the lathe is run, just as a sewing machine is, by foot power. In almost any junk shop or second hand shop you will find an old out-of-date sewing machine for sale. New machines can be bought so cheaply nowadays that a second hand one costs next to nothing.

When you have procured this you must take it to pieces. The wooden top part is fastened to the iron frame by screws from underneath. Take these out, and the top and drawer at the sides may be lifted right off. Then take out the screw at the right hand side of the machine part and slip off the upper belt wheel. This upper belt wheel, the belt, the lower belt wheel, and the iron framework of the machine are all that will be needed for the lathe, and the rest you may discard, or put away in the "handy" pile for some future construction. The lower belt wheel is of course fastened to the frame, so that does not need to be disturbed.

Next get a piece of hickory or some other hard wood twelve inches wide, three feet long and one-and-one-half inches thick. Cut a long, narrow slot in this from one end as is shown in Fig. 1. Then fasten this piece to the top of the iron frame with the same screws that fastened the top of the machine on before. The solid end of the wood should project two inches beyond the right-hand end of the frame where the belt is, and the slotted end will of course extend somewhat beyond the frame at the left. This is what is called the "bed" of the lathe. Now bore the two holes which the belt goes through.

When this is done, measure the hole in the center of the upper belt wheel, where the shaft went through. It will probably be one half inch in diameter. Then get a piece of gas pipe twelve inches long and of the same diameter, outside measurement, as the hole, so that the wheel may be put on it with a "drive fit." This simply means that the wheel fits so tightly that it must be driven on and, once on, it will not turn. It should be driven on far enough so that when the groove for the belt is in line with the groove on the lower belt wheel, the pipe will project the half inch beyond the solid end of the bed.

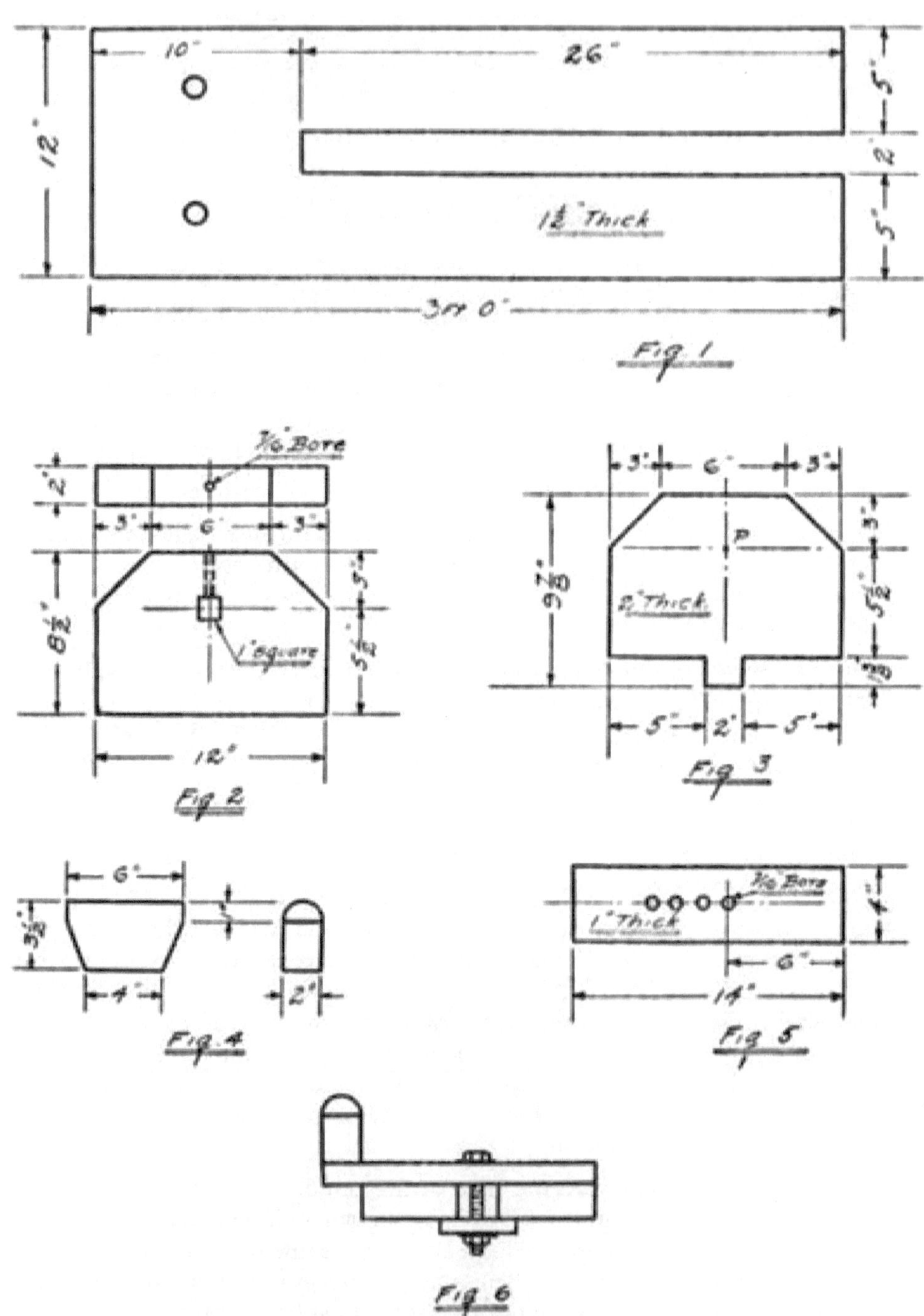

Diagrams of a Turning Lathe.

Now you must make two supports, or "head blocks" for this. Cut from two-inch-thick hard wood two pieces like Fig. 2. The square hole is for the gas pipe to go through and must have a bearing fitted into it. Of course it would be easier to cut just a round hole slightly larger than the pipe for it to turn in, but this bearing, with much turning, would wear loose. So a one-inch square hole is cut; the gas pipe, with a piece of newspaper wrapped around it, is held in the exact center of the hole, the head block standing upright; and melted Babbitt metal is poured down through the hole in the top of the block. To do this pieces of cardboard should be fitted over the pipe and tacked to either side of the block, so that the space inside is like a mold. The metal which remains in the top hole forms a key to hold it. The Babbitt metal may be bought at a hardware store in small bars and melted in a kettle in the fire. It hardens quickly and when hard, the pipe may be removed, the paper taken off and you will have a permanent, durable bearing.

Slip one of these head blocks on the pipe from each end, with an iron washer on each side of each block. The right hand block should be "flush" with the end of the bed, the pipe projecting a half inch beyond it. The other block should be spaced two inches back from the ends of the slot in the bed. The blocks are fastened to the bed with long wood screws which come up through the bed from underneath, and they are held in position on the gas pipe by making "prick punch" holes through the pipe close to the washers and using either "cotter pins" or bent wire through these. Then the end of the pipe, which projects over the slot should be filed so that it has four points, or teeth. This completes the head of the lathe, and is much the most complicated part.

The rest of the lathe consists of a "tail block" and a tool rest, both of which are adjustable to any position desired. Fig. 3 shows the tail block. Like the head blocks, it is made of two-inch thick stock. The bottom of it is cut to slide back and forth in the slot. Just underneath it, on the under side of the bed, is a piece of wood four inches by two inches and one-inch thick which is fastened to the tail block by a screw through the center and which clamps the block in position at any required distance. At the point marked "P" a "lag" screw, which is simply a wood screw with a sharp point and a large flat head, is screwed through the block. The piece of wood to be turned is held in place by this lag screw and the filed teeth on the gas pipe.

The pieces of the tool rest are shown in Fig. 4 and Fig. 5. Fig. 6 shows it as it looks when it is put together in place on the bed of the lathe.

Fig. 4 shows the tool rest itself—that is, the part upon which the chisel or gouge is steadied for cutting. This is fastened upright upon the end of Fig. 5, which is a standard which extends across the bed and is clamped in place, as the tail block is, to a block underneath, except that, instead of being screwed, it is fastened with a three-eighth inch bolt and nut.

Fig. 7 shows the whole lathe "assembled," or put together with each part marked according to its figure numbers so that you can see just how it goes.

All the material it has required has been:

One old sewing machine.

About fifty cents' worth of hard wood.
One three-inch lag screw.
One three-eighths-inch bolt five inches long, with nut and washer.
Four iron washers for gas pipe.
One foot of gas pipe.
Seven three-inch wood screws.
A few cents' worth of Babbitt metal.

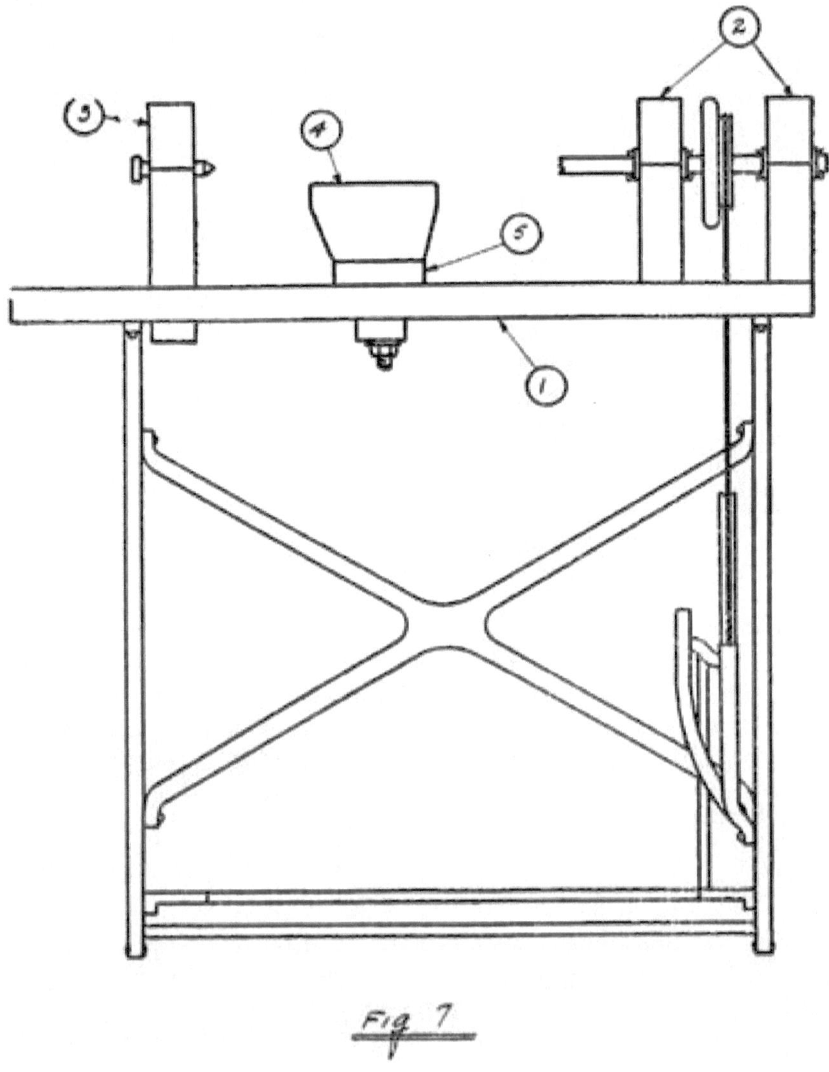

Fig. 7.

The result is a good practical lathe on which anything up to eight inches in diameter and twenty-one inches long may be turned; and I think you'll all agree that it was well worth the making.

HOW TO MAKE A TOY TRAIN

CLEAR the track there! Push the crib over in the corner. Pick up those blocks. Shove the doll's house and blackboard out of the way. Hurry and put the old red candy lantern out of sight. We don't want any danger signals here. The Twentieth Century Limited — the Fast Special of the play room — is coming.

The construction of the Twentieth Century Limited follows close upon *the making of whittling tools*. A little train it is, just an engine, coal car, baggage car, and one passenger coach, but of course there may be any number of additional cars coupled on, provided the train proves popular and the nursery traffic is heavy. The train is made from cigar boxes. The floor of the engine is made from a flat piece of wood, two inches wide by four and one-half inches long, cut perfectly true and then pointed at one end (Fig. 1). Then the cab is made. Fig. 2 shows the front of it — a piece of wood measuring two inches by one and three-quarters, and having two little holes three-eighths of an inch square cut for windows. The side pieces are an inch and a quarter by two inches, cut in the shape of Fig. 3, and each has one little window. The roof is an oblong piece two inches by one and a half. When the whole cab has been nailed together, it is placed in position on the floor of the engine, about a quarter of an inch from the rear end, and nailed there. For the boiler you can use one of mother's basting thread spools. Chip off the ends, making them even with the part where the thread was wound, and then nail it to the floor from underneath. A spot on the upper side of the boiler is smoothed off, and a tiny spool is glued on for a smoke stack. The forward wheels are made from circular pieces an inch in diameter, and the "drivers" from pieces an inch and a half in diameter. Then there are bearings for the wheels, like Fig. 4, those for the smaller wheels being an inch long, and those for the larger wheels three-quarters of an inch in length. They are glued to each side of the floor piece and the axles, made from lollypop sticks, are slipped through. These are cut three inches long, which allows plenty of room for the wheels to turn, and for a little nail to be put through like a cotter pin, to hold them on.

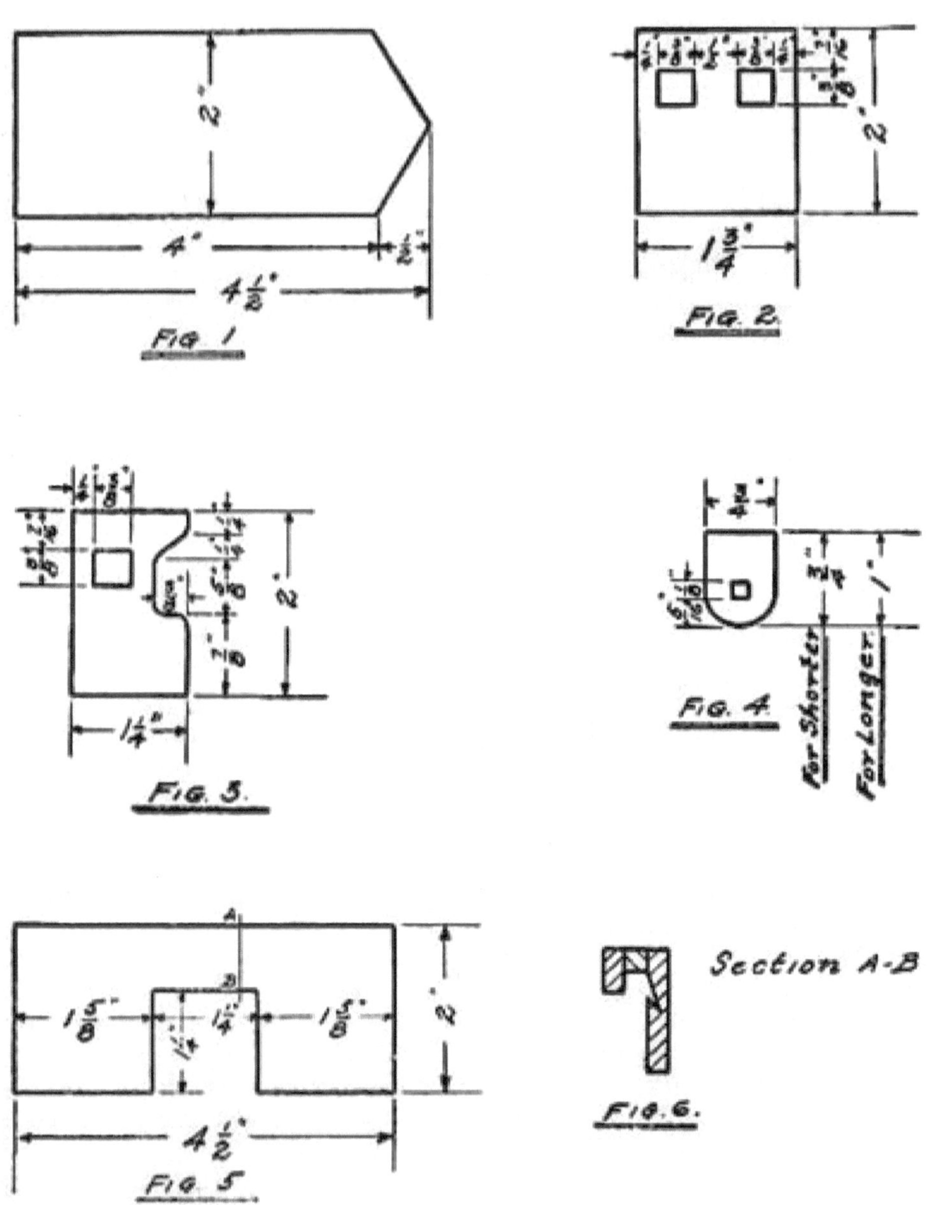

Diagrams of a Toy Train.

The coal car floor measures two inches square, the sides two inches by one, and the ends one and three-quarters by one. These are nailed together to form a little box, and four wheels and bearings like the forward ones on the engine are made. The couplings are made from little round brass hooks, the one on the forward end of each car being horizontal, and the one in the rear end perpendicular.

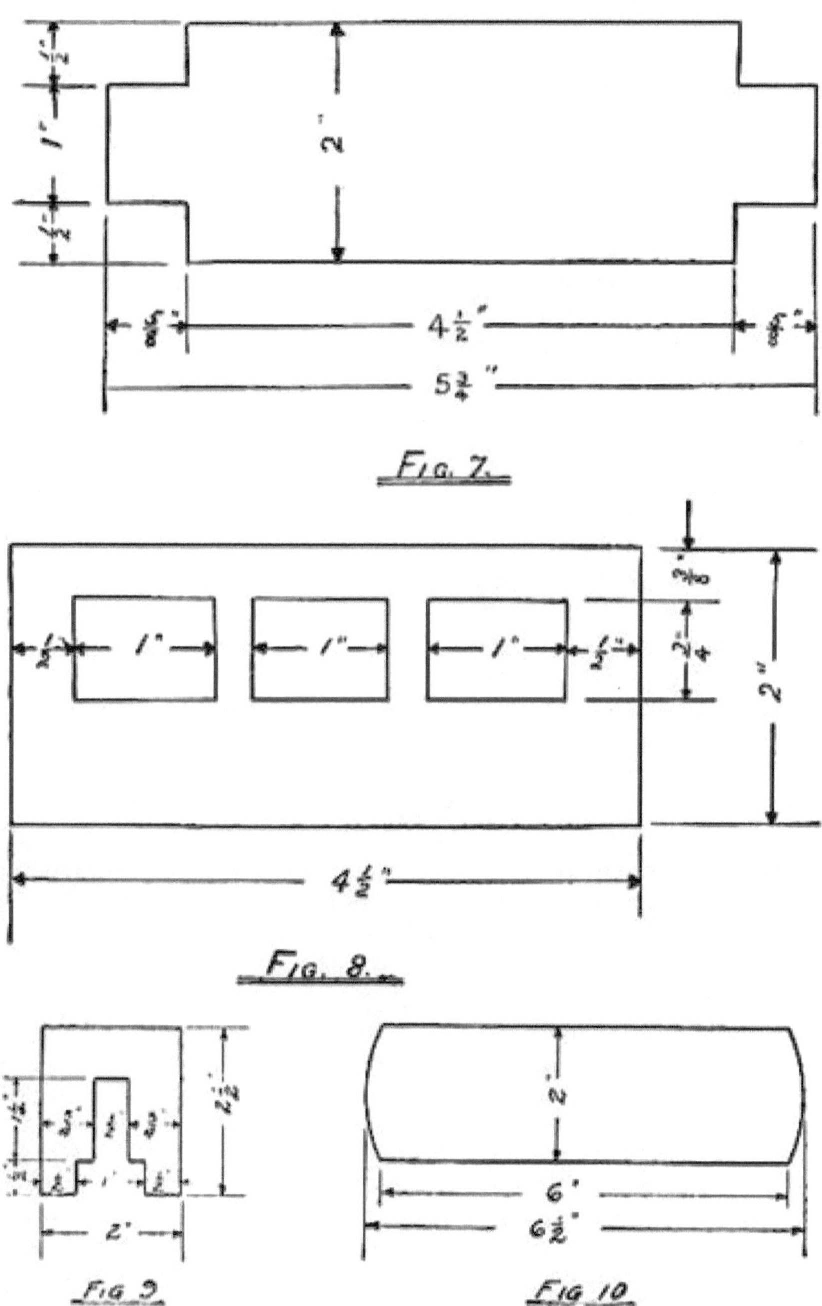

Diagrams of a Toy Train.

The baggage car is a triumph of whittling, for it has a door that will slide back and forth just like a real one. The bottom and top of the car are oblong pieces of wood two inches by four and a half, and the end pieces measure two by two and a quarter inches. The sides are made like Fig. 5, with an opening an inch and a quarter square for a doorway. On the inside of the side pieces, extending to within a half inch of each end, and starting about an eighth of an inch from the top a groove is cut, the depth of the groove being about a quarter of an inch. The door itself is one and thirteen-sixteenths inches high by two inches wide, and has two very small, flat-headed, wood screws, screwed in near the top at an angle, so that the heads rest in this groove, and slide back and forth. Above the door is a strip of wood an eighth of an inch wide, and outside of this another strip a quarter of an inch wide, both of which are nailed in position, and keep the door from slipping out of the groove. Another screw forms a handle for the door, and when the car is put together it is not at all apparent how the door slides. Fig. 6 is a section cut through the side, above the doorway, and shows the groove and how the strips are put on.

For the passenger car the floor is made first—like Fig. 7—the car floor itself measuring two inches by four and one-half, with a projection one inch by five-eighths at each end for a platform. The sides of the car (Fig. 8), are two inches by four and a half, with three holes one inch wide by three-quarters high for Pullman windows. The ends of the car are like Fig. 9. They are slipped over the platforms, the space one and one quarter inch by a half inch forming a doorway and the lower ends extending below the platform to form the side of the steps. The end of the platform is a piece measuring one inch by two inches, and is nailed in position so that the lower edge of it is even with the lower edge of the side pieces, the remainder of it extending above the platform for a railing. There are two steps on each side at each end—eight steps in all. The bottom ones measure a quarter of an inch wide and three-quarters of an inch long, while the upper ones are the same width, but only a half inch long, for they have to fit in between the ends of the car, and the ends of the platform. The roof of the car is like Fig. 10—a piece two inches by six and one-half inches with rounded ends, extending well over the platforms. Both the passenger and baggage cars have wheels exactly like the coal car. When these are done the train is coupled, and away she speeds. "Clear the track there! The Twentieth Century Limited is just pulling into Chicago, and she has made the trip from New York in eighteen hours."

OUT-DOOR TOYS

THIS set of whittled outdoor toys ought to please almost any boy. With kite and fish line time coming soon and the wind blowing a gale for your weather vane, and the other fellows out ready to play "cat" — well, let's see how to make all these toys.

The kite stick in Fig. 1 is made from a piece of pine wood eight inches long, and, roughly cut out, about three-quarters of an inch square. This is smoothed down to five-eighths of an inch, and then you start in to make it round. First the four corners of the square are trimmed off evenly for the full length, making it an eight-sided stick, and then these corners are again trimmed, until finally the stick is round enough to be sandpapered smooth. It is better to draw a five-eighth inch circle on each end of the stick before you trim it down, so that you can see whether you are making a true round. When the line for the bevel is marked around one-eighth of an inch from the ends, the bevel is cut, the notch is cut around the middle, and the stick is ready to tie your kite string to.

For the reel in Fig. 2 and also the weather vane in Fig. 7, it is better to select a piece of wood which is already "dressed" — that is, finished smooth to the thickness you require, because it is hard to make a broad surface true with a jack knife. Cigar boxes are three-sixteenths of an inch thick, and a piece of one will make a good, stout reel. In making all of these toys, the pattern should be drawn on the wood as far as possible with pencil, scale, and straight edge, before any cutting is done. The reel should be cut first into an oblong, two and a quarter inches by four and a quarter, then the corners are rounded so that the line will not catch on them, and lastly the "recessed edge" where the line is to be wound is made, cutting from each end of the opening toward the center, and gradually working it down even.

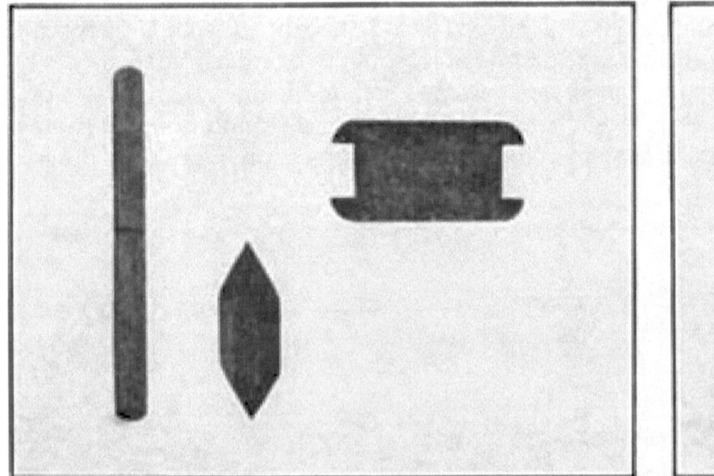
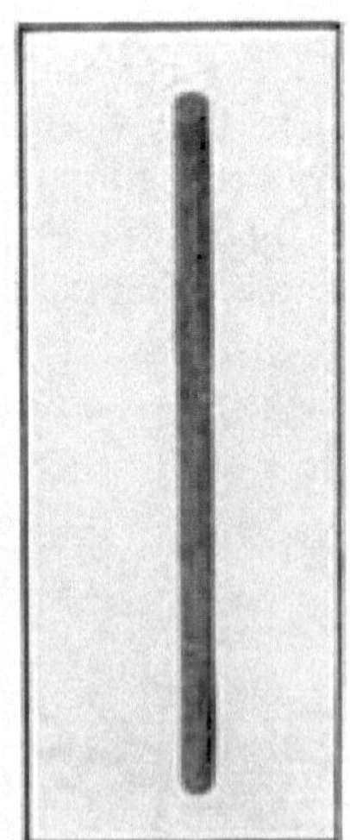

(A) Whittled Weather Vane., (B) Kite Stick; "Cat"; Reel for Fish Line., (C) "Cat" Stick.

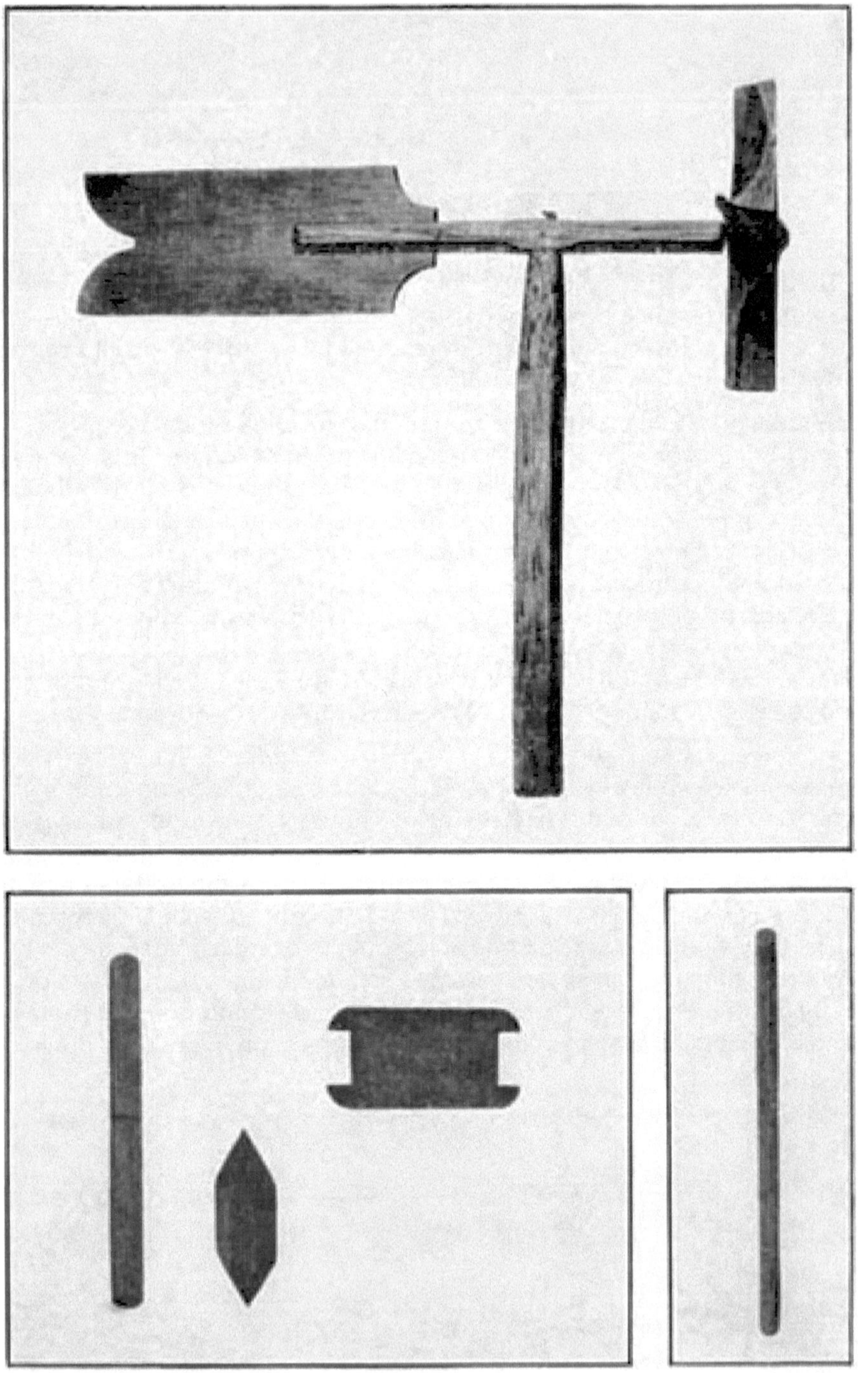

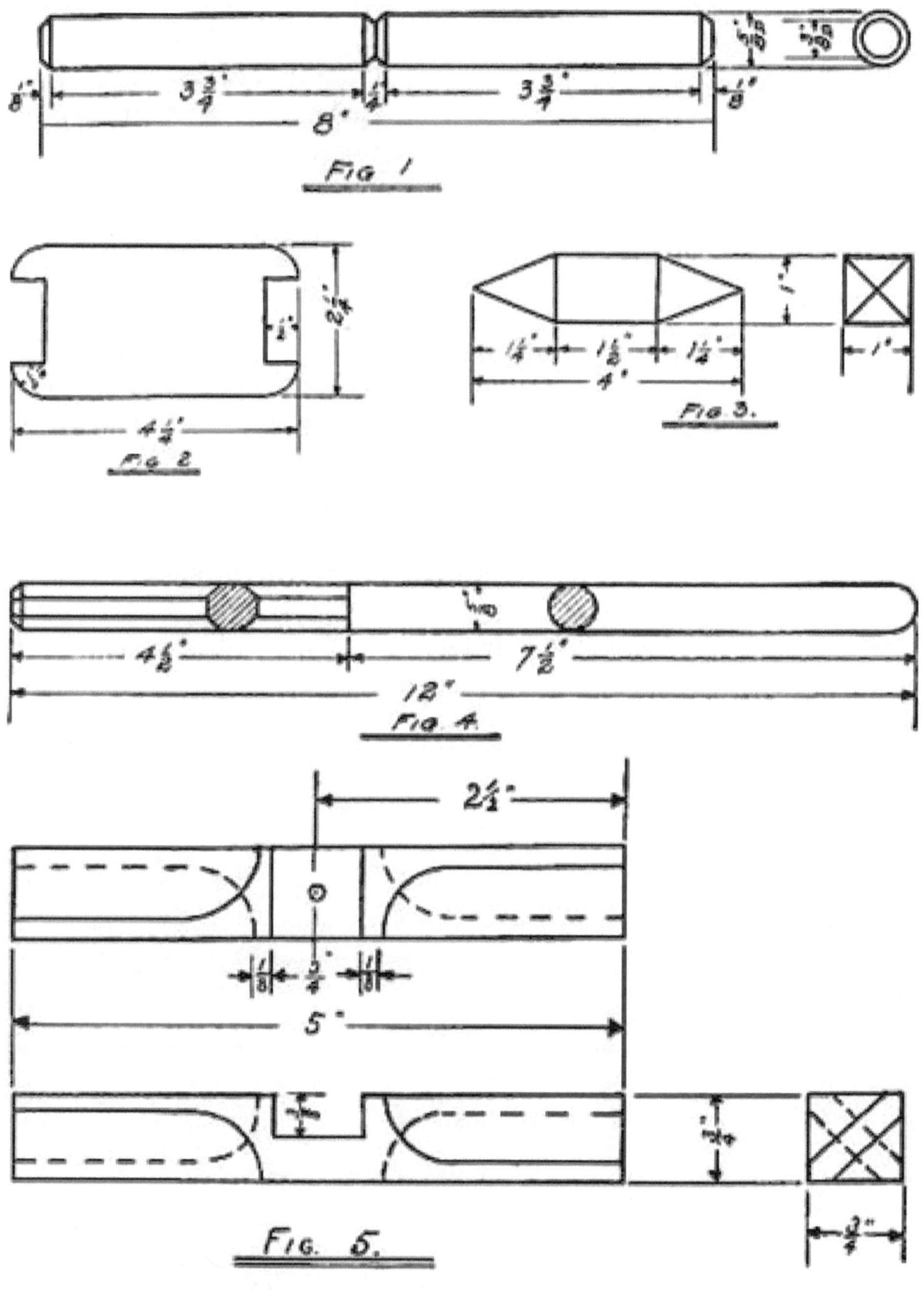

Diagrams of a Kite Stick, Reel, "Cat," "Cat" Stick, and Weather Vane.

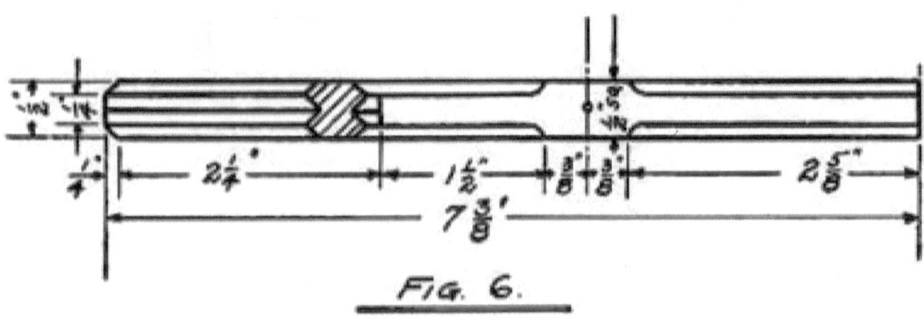

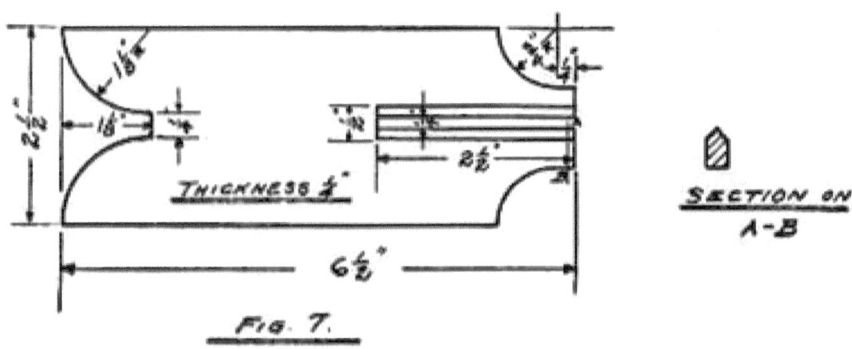

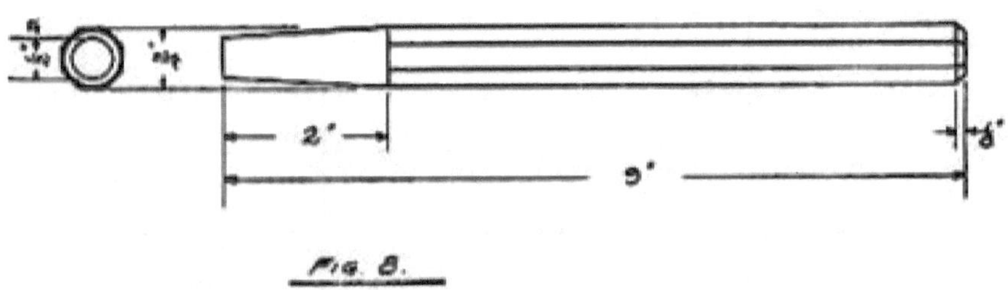

Diagrams of a Weather Vane.

There are not many boys who don't know how to play "cat." It requires a good deal of skill, and if you don't break anybody's window or put out anybody's eye, it's a lot of fun. It requires two boys to play this game. You lay the cat down flat—as in Fig. 3—and, with the stick (Fig. 4), held by the octagonal end, hit the cat sharply on one end, and as it flies up bat it forward. It is up to the other fellow to catch it, and if he does, it counts you out, and gives him a turn. But if he doesn't catch it, you measure with the stick, end over end from where you stand to where the cat has fallen, and that counts so many points for you. Then the other fellow has another chance to count you out by throwing the cat from where it fell and trying to hit your stick. If it falls short or goes beyond, you again measure the distance with your stick, and that too counts in your favor.

The cat is made from a piece of pine four inches long and an inch square. The center section is marked off and then a line is drawn exactly across the middle of each end—not diagonally, but straight up and down. The sides are slanted down to this line, like a wedge, and then the other two sides are slanted to the middle point at each end. The wood for the stick is twelve inches long and five-eighths of an inch square, and is worked down just as the kite stick was, except that the handle is left eight sided, while the rest is made round. The octagon and circle which are shown with parallel diagonal lines on them are "cross sections" and show what the stick would look like if it were cut straight through at that point.

The weather vane is the hardest toy to make. Fig. 5 shows three views of one piece of the wheel—a top view, a front view, and an end view,—just as though you looked at the piece in front and then squarely at the top, and then turned it around and looked at the end. A piece of wood three-quarters of an inch square by five inches long is used for this, and two of them are made and fitted together—making a wheel with four arms. It is better to cut the section for the joint first, for the wood is less apt to split before it has been weakened by any other cutting. This is a similar cutting to that in the reel, except that the grain lies in the opposite direction, and the cutting should be done from the center of the opening toward each end. Then opposite corners are slanted down so that the ends of the arms are thin and aslant to catch the wind, as the end view shows. The dotted lines are the edges which are not visible. After the two pieces are fitted together a two-inch nail is driven through both and into the end of Fig. 6, which is not beveled. It should be turned around until it works loosely and will turn easily in the wind.

The stick in Fig. 6 is seven and three-eighths inches long by a half inch square. After the section three-quarters of an inch long, where the nail hole is shown, and which remains square, is marked off, the rest of the stick is made eight sided. Then the eight-inch bevel shown on the end is cut, and, for a distance of two and a half inches from that end, a V-shaped groove is cut on two opposite sides. This end of the stick is to slide into the opening in the end of the wing (Fig. 7). Another two-inch nail joins this piece to the upright stick (Fig. 8) and forms a pivot for it to swing around on. The wing is a flat piece six and a half inches long by two and a half wide. The curves are laid out with a compass (R. in the measurements denotes radius) and the $2\frac{1}{2}$"-opening is made as shown in one end. The little cross-section shows how it is cut to a pointed edge which slides into the groove in Fig. 6.

The upright stick is nine inches long by three-quarters of an inch square, and is worked down similarly to the other sticks, except that the end which is round is tapered from three-quarters to one-half inch. The "break" in the drawing simply means that it is longer than is actually shown. When the windmill is fitted together and put out where it will catch the wind, a boy will find that it was well worth making.

HOW TO MAKE YOUR OWN DESK SET

A DESK set is a great addition to a boy's desk. If he has a pen tray he knows where his pencils and pens are to be found without rummaging through a tangled mess of top strings and marble bags and nails. If he puts away on the bill file that *I Owe You* that Billy Smith gave him for a pair of rabbits, it won't be all crumpled up and beyond identification when Billy gets his next month's allowance. When you come to think of it, a desk set has a great many advantages—and then, there's the fun of making it.

The desk set which is shown in the picture comprises five pieces—an ink well stand, a bill file, a pen tray, an envelope opener, and a book rack. It is all, with the exception of the envelope opener, made of one-eighth-inch basswood.

For the ink well stand (Fig. 1) use a piece of wood, four inches square. The two-and-a-half-inch opening—which is the size of the average glass ink well—should be cut first, before the corners are weakened by cutting out the half-inch rounds. After this is done, cut the corners, and last, the eight-inch bevel. Fig. 2 shows one of the feet of the ink well. It is shown, by dotted lines, in position in Fig. 1. The four feet are glued to the bottom of Fig. 1 and the inside corners project inside the opening, making four half-inch squares on which the ink well may rest. The feet are made from pieces of wood one and seven-eighths inches square, cut in the shape shown, and ornamented with a little design in "chip" carving. This chip carving is ordinarily done with what is called a skew chisel—that is, a chisel which is not square at the end, but which has one point an eighth of an inch or more longer than the other, so that when it is put into the wood, one end of the cut will be deep while the other is barely cut out at all. However, it may be done with a jack knife, if you are very careful. In the "motif" shown in Fig. 2, the points where the three lines from adjoining corners meet are where the deepest part of the cuts should be. This is done with the knife held point down and the thumb on the end of the handle. Then, with the knife still in the same position in the hand, you chip out the wood with a sliding cut toward you, slanting it down to the depth of the cut. It is a little difficult to describe this without seeing it done, but if you look at the patterns and the photographs, and experiment a little on a piece of wood, you will find it easy.

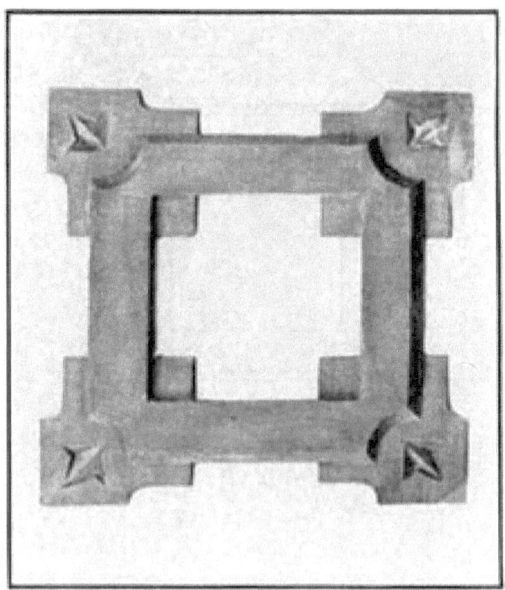

(A) File., (B) Ink Well., (C) Pen Tray.

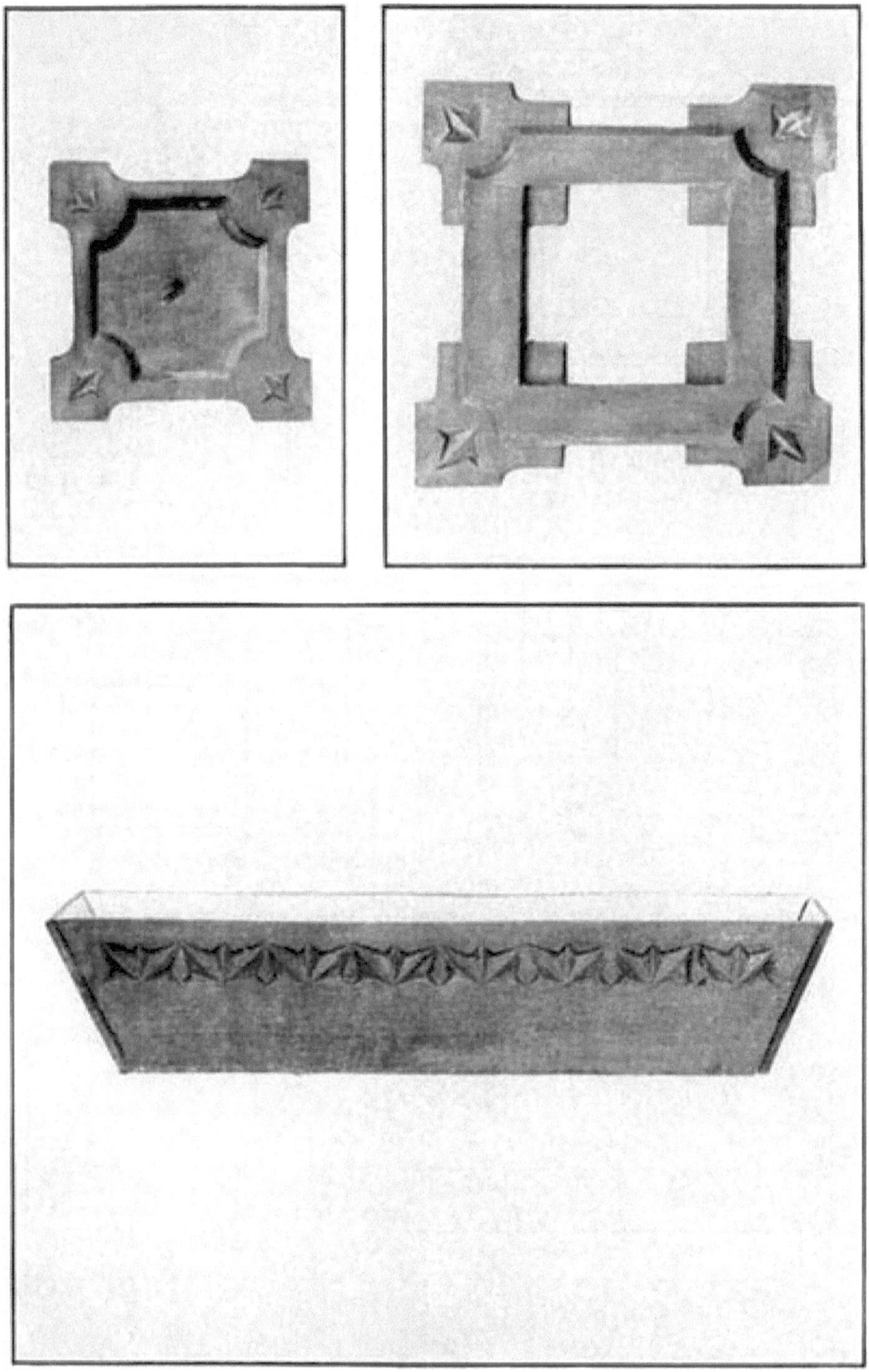

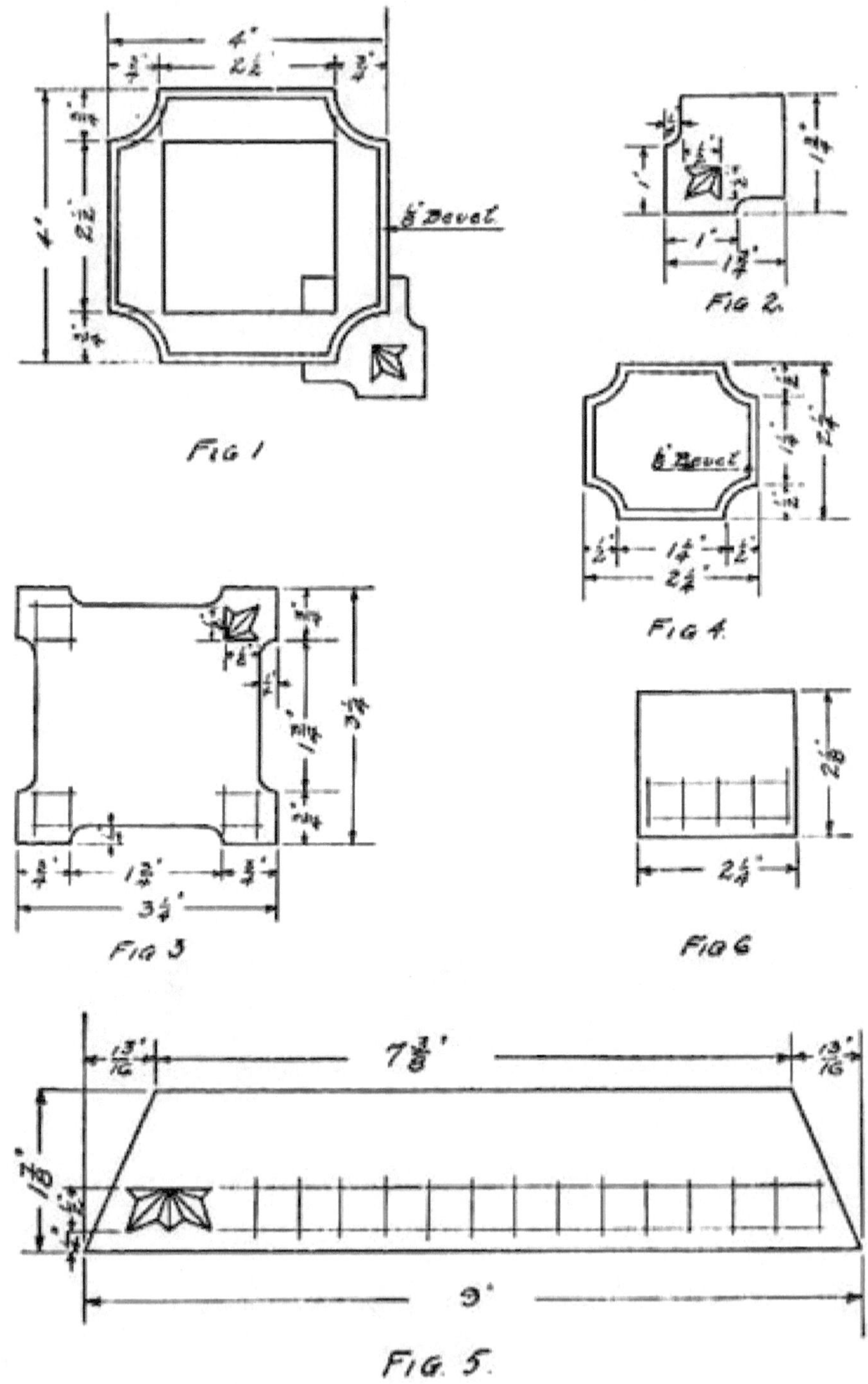

Diagrams of an Ink Well Stand, a Bill File and a Pen Tray.

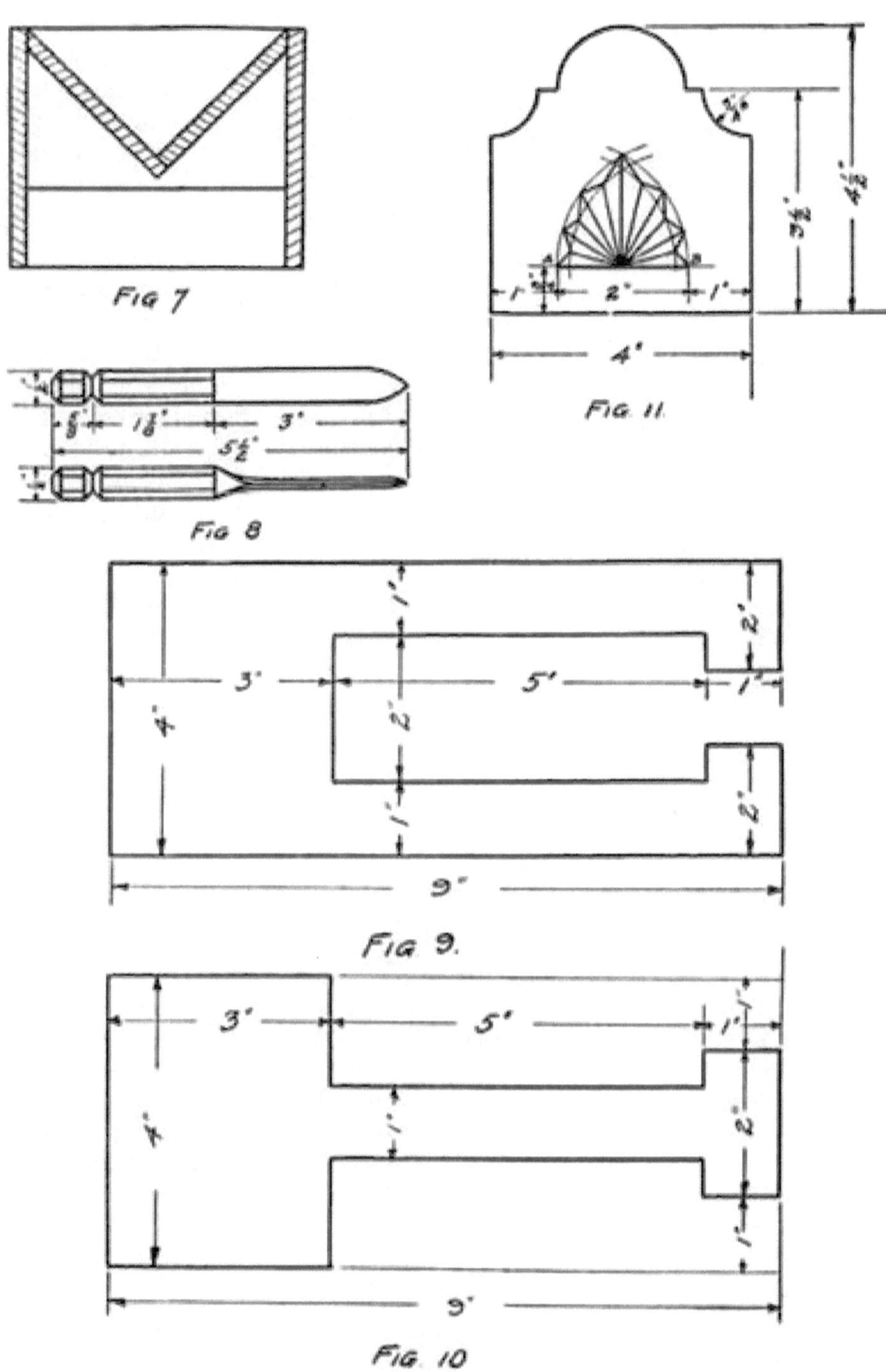

Diagrams of a Pen Tray, an Envelope Opener and a Book Rack.

Fig. 3 and Fig. 4 show the bill file. Fig. 3 is made from a three and a quarter-inch square, cut similarly to the foot of the ink well, and with the same motif carved on each corner. It should be remembered in cutting the recessed edges that the sides running *with* the grain must be cut *from* each end, and the cross-cut sides cut *toward* each end. Fig. 4 is cut like Fig. 1, except that there is no opening in it. It is then glued to the top of Fig. 3, and a three-inch nail is driven up through the center.

Fig. 5 shows one side of the pen tray. It is made from a piece of wood nine inches long at the bottom, tapered to seven and three-eighths inches at the top, and one and seven-eighth inches wide. The motif for the carving is made by putting together two of the squares shown in Fig. 2 and then repeating this again and again. It makes a very pretty and effective decoration. Fig. 6 is one of the end pieces, and is decorated in the same way. Fig. 7 is a cross-section showing the construction of the pen tray. For this you should first make two oblongs, seven and three-eighth inches long, one of them being one and three-eighths, and the other, one and one-half inches wide. These are fastened together at right angles, the long one topping over the shorter, with tiny nails. Then a piece measuring two inches by one and one-quarter is nailed to each end, to hold the tray firm. Next, the top edge all around is beveled—the side edges, so that the sides (Fig. 5) may be fitted on straight up and down, and the ends, at such an angle that they will not interfere in putting on the end pieces (Fig. 6). Then the sides and ends are glued in position, and the tray is finished.

For the envelope opener in Fig. 8, a piece of gumwood five and a half inches long by a half inch square is used. For two and a half inches from the end it is reduced to an octagonal shape. Then the notches are cut, and the end of the handle—four sides only, not the entire eight—beveled. Then the blade is cut, curving down from the handle, and reducing the blade to an even thickness of an eighth of an inch. When this is quite even the end is pointed, and the entire outside edge of the blade is beveled down from both sides, to a cutting edge.

The base of the book rack (Figs. 9 and 10), is made from two pieces of wood measuring four inches by nine, which are cut as shown, to fit and slide within each other. It measures thirteen inches, closed, and sixteen inches, open. A good way to fasten the pieces together so that they will slide easily and yet be firm, is with strips of thin sheet brass, which can be bought very cheaply. A strip three-quarters of an inch wide is passed around the rack at D with both pieces in position, lapped and fastened to D. Another similar piece is passed around at C and fastened to C. Then the ends (Fig. 11) are made. This requires two pieces four inches wide by four and a half long, with the grain running up and down. The top is made a little prettier by a semi-circular curve and a reverse quarter circle at each side of it. The deep carving is a trifle more elaborate than on the other things, and must be done carefully where the cuts all meet at the bottom.

After measuring and finding the position of the points "a" and "b" you should use these as centers from which to make the curves which determine the outline of your design. The cutting is done exactly as you did before. When these are finished they should be fastened on top of the base, at either end, with little brass hinges on the inside. A strip of wood four inches long by three-quarters of an inch wide is placed at the lower edge of the end pieces, on the outside, for added strength, and the screws fastening the hinges will hold it in place.

Book Rack.

This completes the actual making of the desk set. It may be sandpapered, or it may be varnished, or, if you are fortunate enough to have a mission desk, it may be stained to match. In any case it is worth having.

WILD ANIMALS YOU CAN MAKE

W ITH a circus folder or animal book for a copy, a few old cigar boxes, and a jack knife, a very lively and life-like menagerie can be made.

Cut the cigar boxes apart, and sandpaper the pieces very smooth. Then take a pencil and sketch as well as you can the animals in the pictures — at least the bodies of them, for the legs are to be attached afterward, so that they can stand and "do things."

The cutting must be done very, very carefully, for the outlines make so many different angles with the grain of the wood. It is not in the least like straight cutting with the grain, or even straight cross-cutting, and the wood has an irritating habit of splitting off some vital part of the animal's anatomy.

It is impossible to make the tails out of wood, so they are made of heavy string, glued in place. For the monkey, you can make a tail of wire, so that he can swing by it.

Make the legs of the animals separately and fasten them on to the bodies with tiny nails. Place the two fore legs or two hind legs in position on either side of the body piece, and drive through them a short wire nail, a very little longer than is necessary to go through the three thicknesses of wood. Then rest the head of the nail on a piece of iron, and hammer the point, forming a little rivet to pivot the legs. The feet must also be made separately, and fastened on in the same way, so that, whatever position the legs are in, the feet will remain level.

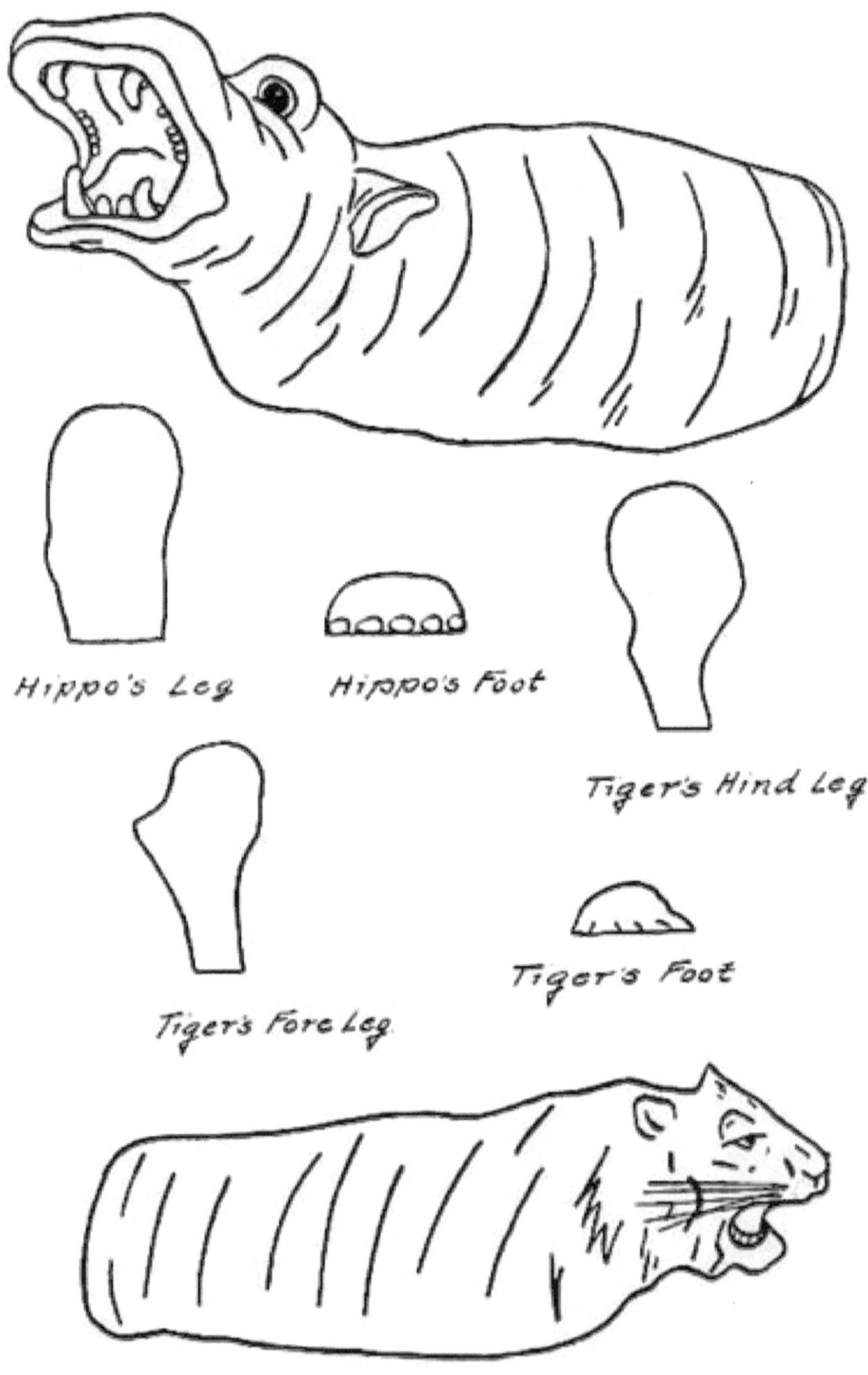

Patterns of Hippo and Tiger.

Whittled Wild Animals Giraffe, Camel.

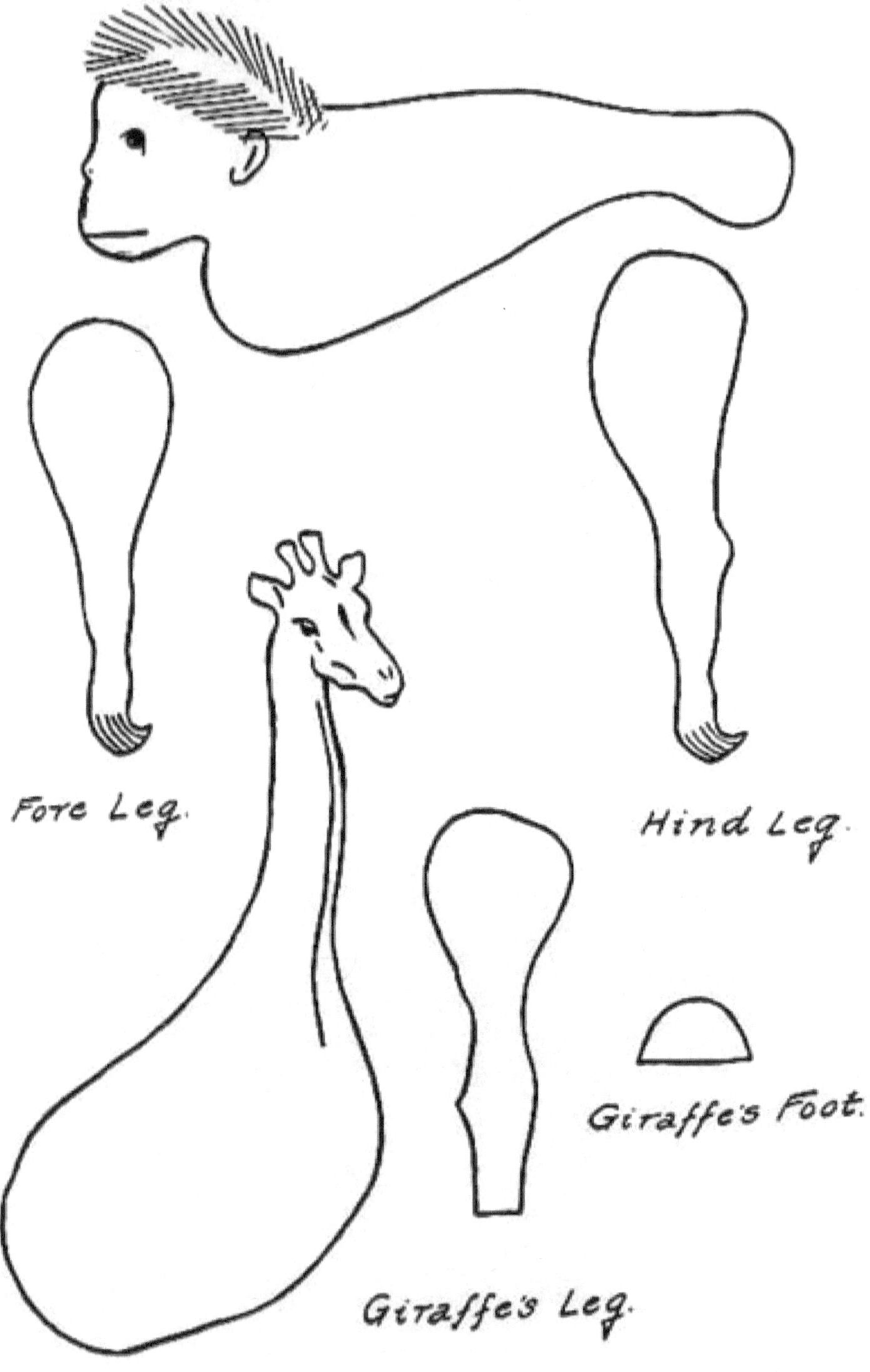

Patterns of Monkey and Giraffe.

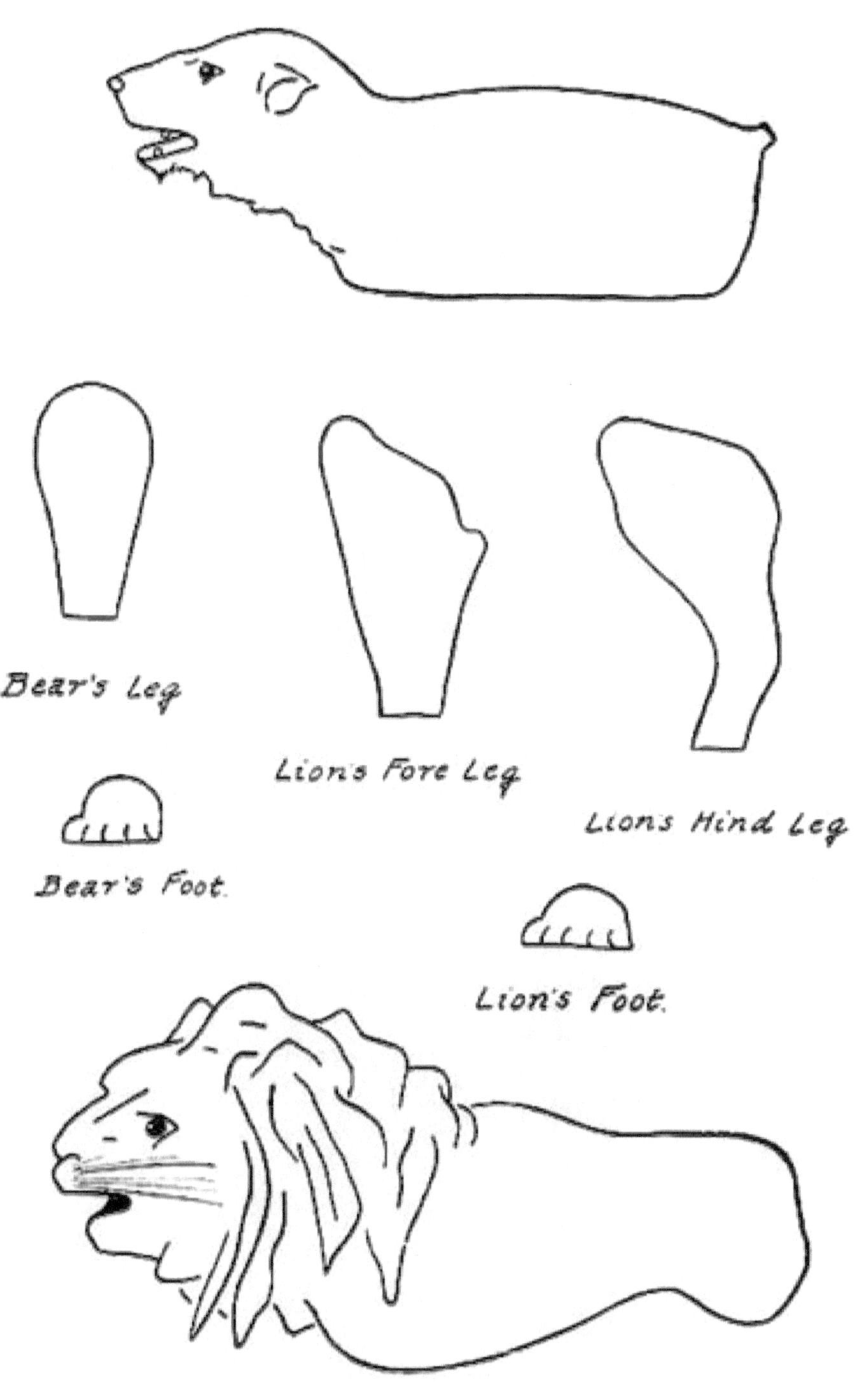

Patterns of Bear and Lion.

Whittled Wild Animals Bear, Lion, "Darwin".

HOW TO MAKE A SET
OF MISSION FURNITURE

A VERY attractive set of furniture suitable for a doll's nursery, may be whittled from pieces of old cigar boxes. It consists of four pieces—a "Craftsman" bed, a chair, a table, and a chest of drawers.

For the head of the bed take a piece of wood four inches square, and, placing it with the grain of the wood running up and down, mark it out like Fig. 1. As a general rule, the grain of the wood should lie with the longest dimension, but in all the upright pieces of this set it must run up and down. Outline first the "recessed edge," which forms the legs of the bed, scoring it lightly with the point of the knife. Then cutting a little bit out at a time, and working from the center toward each end, bring it down to the line. The two openings, an eighth of an inch by a half inch, for the joints, must be cut with the point of the knife—the ends first, then the sides, and lastly the wood is chipped out, and the opening is evened up. The foot of the bed is identical with the head except that is three inches high instead of four.

Next come the side pieces—two pieces seven inches long and one inch wide, cut like Fig. 2. The half-inch ends slide through the openings in the head and foot of the bed, and fasten with little wedge-shaped pegs like Fig. 5. Inside each of these side pieces, and "flush" with the bottom edge, glue a strip cut like Fig. 3, and fit in five little slats three and three-eighths inches long by a half inch wide (Fig. 4). Then, to complete it and make it look as much like a Craftsman bed as possible, paste on the head a panel of light brown wrapping paper, on which are four little conventional kittens, painted in Van Dyke brown.

The top of the table (Fig. 6) is a piece four inches square. The end pieces (Fig. 7) are cut similarly to the head and foot of the bed, with the same recessed edge and the same openings, varying only in the outside dimensions. The sides too (Fig. 8), are similar to the sides of the bed, except that they are of course, much shorter. Slip them through the openings in the end pieces, fasten them with four little pegs, glue the top on, and the table is done.

Dolls' Chair and Table, Whittled in Mission Style.

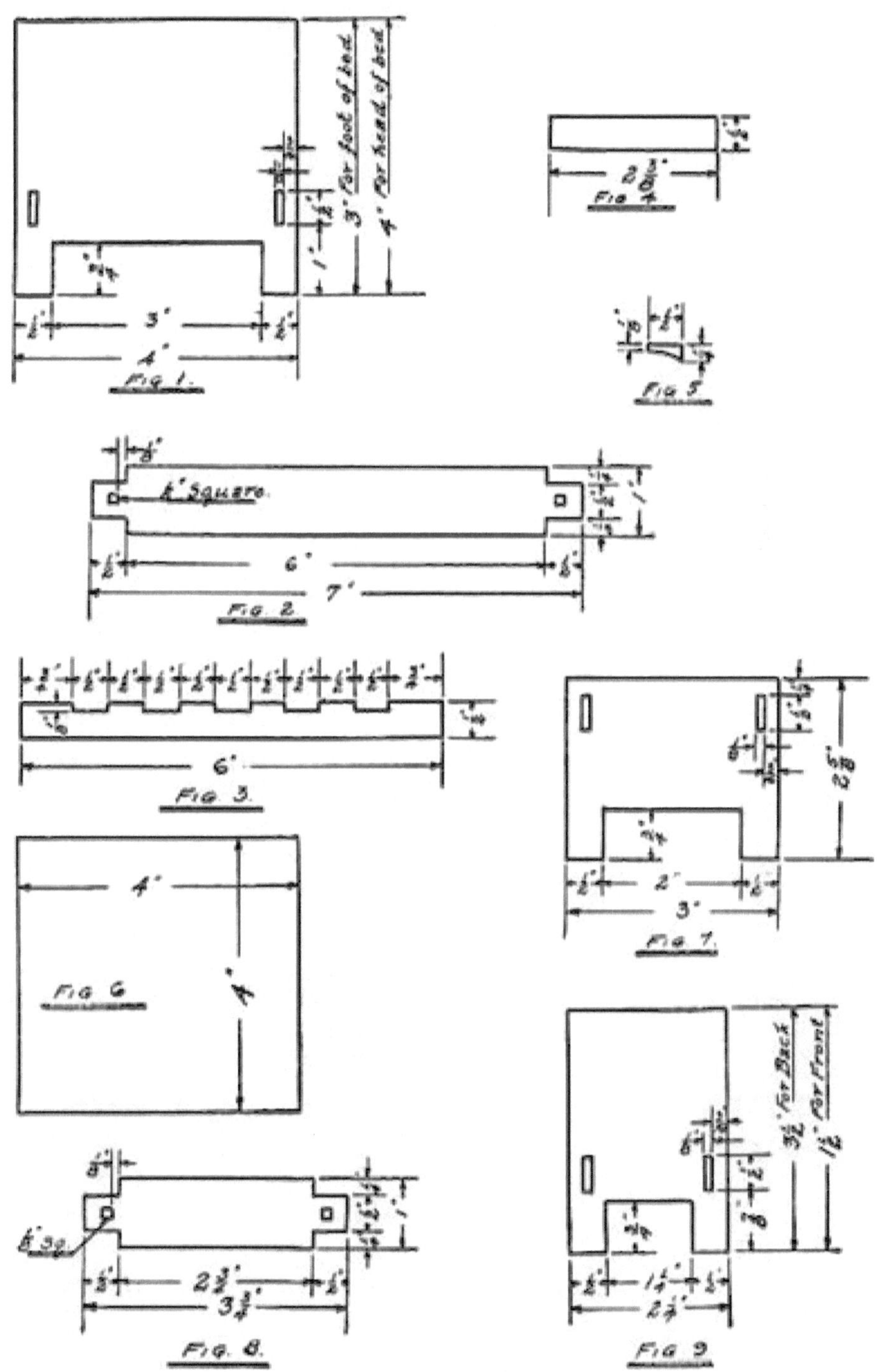

Diagrams of a "Craftsman" Bed, a Table and a Chair.

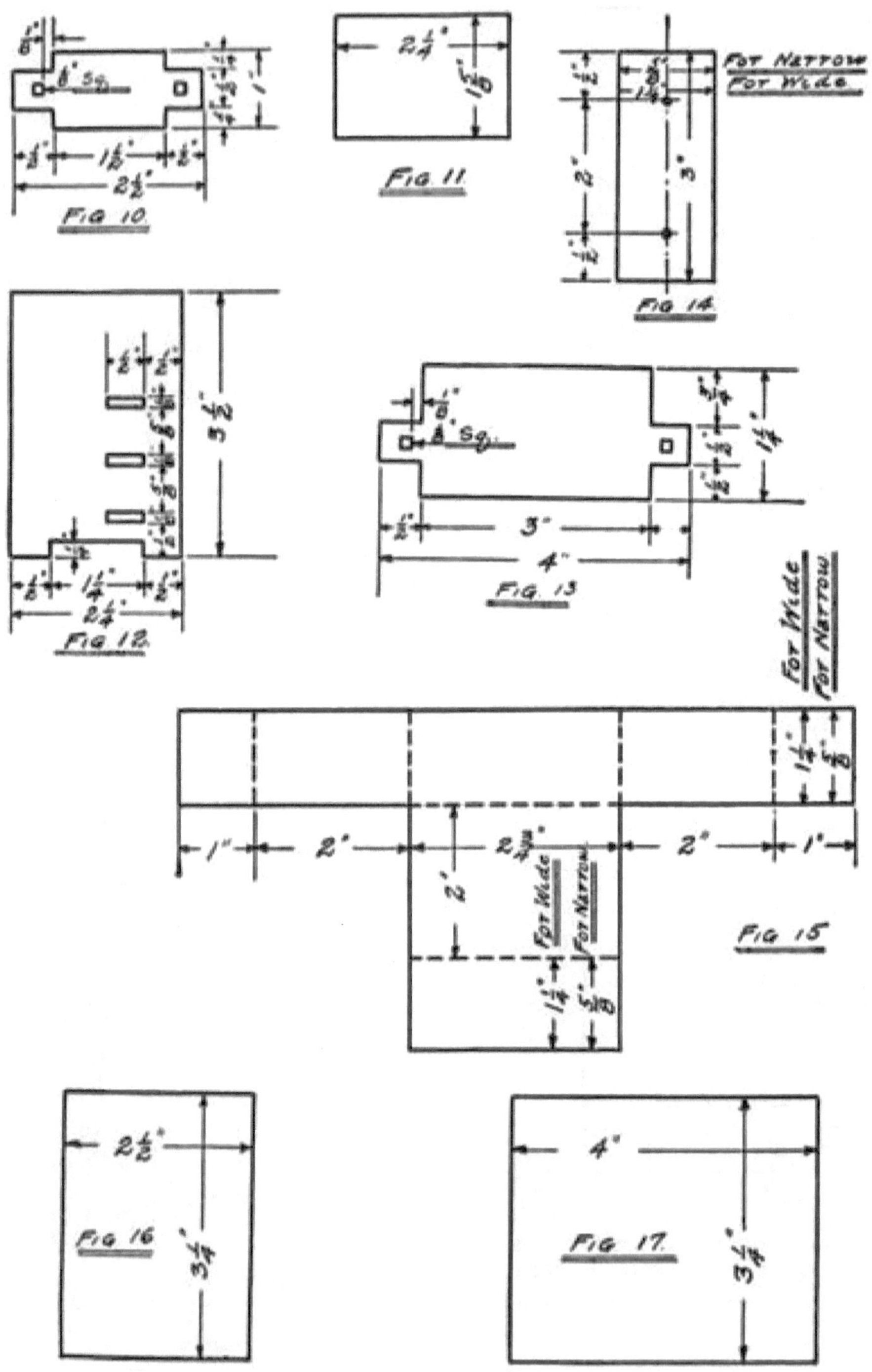

Diagrams of a Chair and a Chest of Drawers.

The chair is built on the same general lines as the table and bed. The chair back (Fig. 9) measures two and a quarter inches wide by three and one-half inches high, while the front upright piece is exactly similar but only an inch and one-half high—just high enough for dolly to swing her feet comfortably. When these and the side pieces (Fig. 10) are done and put together, glue on a piece one and five-eighths inches by two and a quarter (Fig. 11) for the seat.

The construction of the chest of drawers is a little more elaborate. Make first two side pieces like Fig 12. They measure two and a quarter inches wide by three and one-half high, and have a recessed edge a quarter of an inch deep at the bottom to form feet, and three openings in each side for the partitions between the drawers. There are one deep drawer at the top, and two shallower ones below it. Make three pieces like Fig. 13, four inches long by one and three-quarters wide. The little square and piece for the joint are not exactly in the middle, and the longer space goes toward the back, but is intended to leave a little open space of a half inch at the back.

Next make three pieces for the fronts of the drawers (Fig. 14), two of them five-eighths of an inch wide, and one measuring an inch and a quarter. In each of these make two holes for the knobs. The drawers themselves (Fig. 15) are made of light weight pasteboard. The bottom dimensions remain the same of course for all—two and three-quarter inches by two—but the depths of the sides must be one and one-quarter inches for the wider, and five-eighths of an inch for the narrower ones. When these are cut out, fold them on the dotted lines to form a box, with the sides which lap over each other at the front. The knobs of the drawers are made of large beads. Put a piece of string through each bead, and then push the two ends of string through the hole in the front of the drawer, and through a corresponding hole in the pasteboard drawer itself. Then tie the two ends of string from the right-hand knob to the two pieces from the left-hand knob in a firm square knot, accomplishing the triple purpose of holding the knobs in position, fastening the front piece on to the drawer, and holding the drawer in shape. An oblong piece of wood two and a quarter inches by three and a quarter (Fig. 16) makes the top, and another four inches by three and a quarter forms the back.

Dolls' Whittled Chest of Drawers.

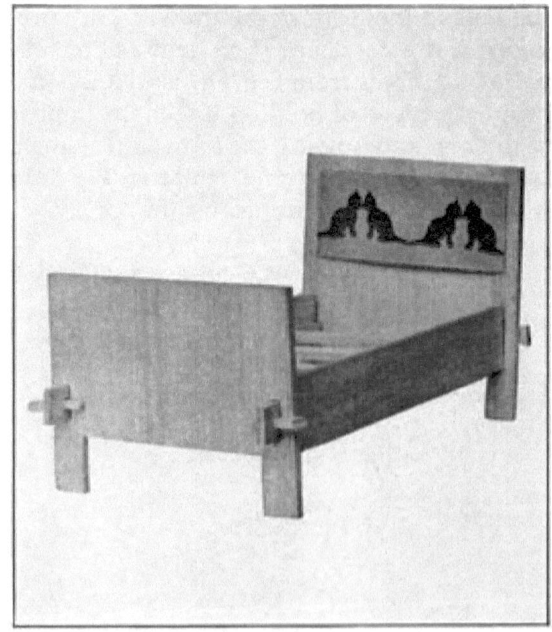

Whittled Dolls' Bed.

TOYS THAT HIDE IN THE WOOD BOX

THE farm barn with its loft hung with cobwebs and the great hay mows, and the farm wagons to scramble out and in is surely a delight to the country boy; but if one corner of the barn has a big pile of clean, smooth blocks and sticks of kindling wood, the charm of the place will be redoubled.

A glance, only, at a heap of ordinary, everyday kindling wood will suggest all sorts of plays to the resourceful boy. With the aid of a few simple tools, a hammer, a light saw, and some wire nails, the pieces of wood may be changed into crude, but realistic toys that will give the little folks quite as much pleasure as any to be found in a toy shop.

Look, first, at the building possibilities of a pile of kindling wood. The long, straight sticks may be balanced on the barn floor to represent a regiment of soldiers. With penciled faces, and soldier caps they make very fine little men; and if there are two opposing armies, a most exciting sham battle may be carried on with horse chestnuts and green apples for ammunition, and a prize for the general whose kindling-wood forces stand up the longest.

A miniature pig pen may be built by piling up kindling-wood sticks in log-cabin fashion. The sticks selected for the pen should be, as nearly as possible, of the same length. Two sticks should be laid parallel. These are then connected by laying other sticks across their ends. The boy should continue building in this manner until the pig pen is of a good height. A very fine, fat pig may be made of a small cucumber, having twigs stuck into his body for legs, one of the vine tendrils for a curly tail and melon seeds for ears.

A log house is constructed by building a foundation similar to the pig pen. The roof is formed by laying a row of sticks, quite close together, across the top. A family of little clothes pin dolls may live most comfortably in a kindling wood house.

In front of the house there should be a strong, rail fence to protect the inmates from any Indians who may come in while the builder is away. To build a Virginia rail fence, two sticks of kindling wood should be crossed in the shape of a letter V. A third stick is added at a similar angle with the second stick. This form of building is continued until the fence is of the required length. Going back to the first stick, a second layer of sticks is started on top of the first layer; and the fence may be built as high as one wishes by the addition of a third and a fourth layer.

There are ever so many playthings that can be built from the wood found in the wood pile. A boy who is clever with his jack knife will be able to make a set of ten pins from sticks of kindling wood by carving little round heads at the ends of the sticks. Very straight bits of wood which will balance well should be chosen for the ten pins. He can also carve quaint wooden dolls for the little sister.

The accompanying illustration shows a toy barnyard that was made by a group of children. Their only tools were a couple of hammers, a toy saw, some nails and a jack knife. The only materials used were found in the wood pile in the wood-shed.

The barnyard fence is constructed from lath. Long strips are used for the bars of the fence. The fence posts are bits of lath, also, carved in six-inch lengths, pointed at the top with a knife, and nailed to the longer strips. Bits of leather are tacked in place for the gate hinges. Bits of kindling wood split into narrow sections are nailed together for the pig pen and the cow shed. Some old wooden boxes are used for the farm wagon and the wheelbarrow, the curved edges of the wheelbarrow being made with a jack knife. The box cover is used as wheel material, two circles being cut out of the soft wood with a jack knife and fastened to the body of the wagon with dowel sticks. Another box is mounted on a standard of lath and forms a very realistic pigeon house. The chicken coops are little wood squares nailed together at an angle of 90° with bits of lath fastened across the front. With the addition of a rude barn made from scraps of wood, a dog house—which is only a small edition of the barn—and a cattle shed, the farmyard is complete—a crude but unfailing source of amusement for many rainy days.

One of the simplest toys to make of wood basket scraps is a little play sled. For this you will need three oblong pieces of wood—one of them (Fig. 1) measuring four inches wide by seven inches long, and the other two (Fig. 2) measuring two and a half inches wide by nine and one-half inches long. Some pieces of an old packing box about a half inch thick will do very nicely for these. Mark the outlines first with a pencil; then cut them out with the saw, and "true them up" with a knife—that is, take off the little roughnesses that the saw has left, and make the edges perfectly straight and square. Next the two long side pieces which you have made must be shaped. Measure off on the lower edge (with the piece standing in position as though it were on the sled), two inches from the front end. Connect this by a line with the upper front corner, and cut it. Then round off the lower end of this cut so that it curves into the bottom. Now make a nail hole near the front end of each side piece for a string to go through, nail the side pieces to the other oblong which you made for the top, and the little sled is done.

Another very simple toy to make of this material is a little chicken coop. This is made of one square piece of wood and another piece which is almost square. The first piece (Fig. 3) measures seven inches each way, and the other one (Fig. 4) measures seven inches in one direction, and in the other direction seven inches less the thickness of the wood. This is because one piece laps over the end of the other, and the end of the first piece forms part of the other side of the coop. When these pieces are cut and made perfectly square and true, lap the longer piece over the end of the shorter so that it will be just even with the surface, and nail in position. For the slats (Fig. 5) cut some strips an inch wide and thinner than the sides of the coop. Lath is good if you have it. Two of these strips are ten inches long, two are seven inches, and two are four inches. The longest ones are nailed across the open sides of the coop, one on each side, an inch above the bottom. The middle-sized ones are nailed two inches above these, and the shortest ones two inches higher. Then the ends of these strips are sawed off almost even with the coop.

Toy Barnyard Made of Kindling Wood.

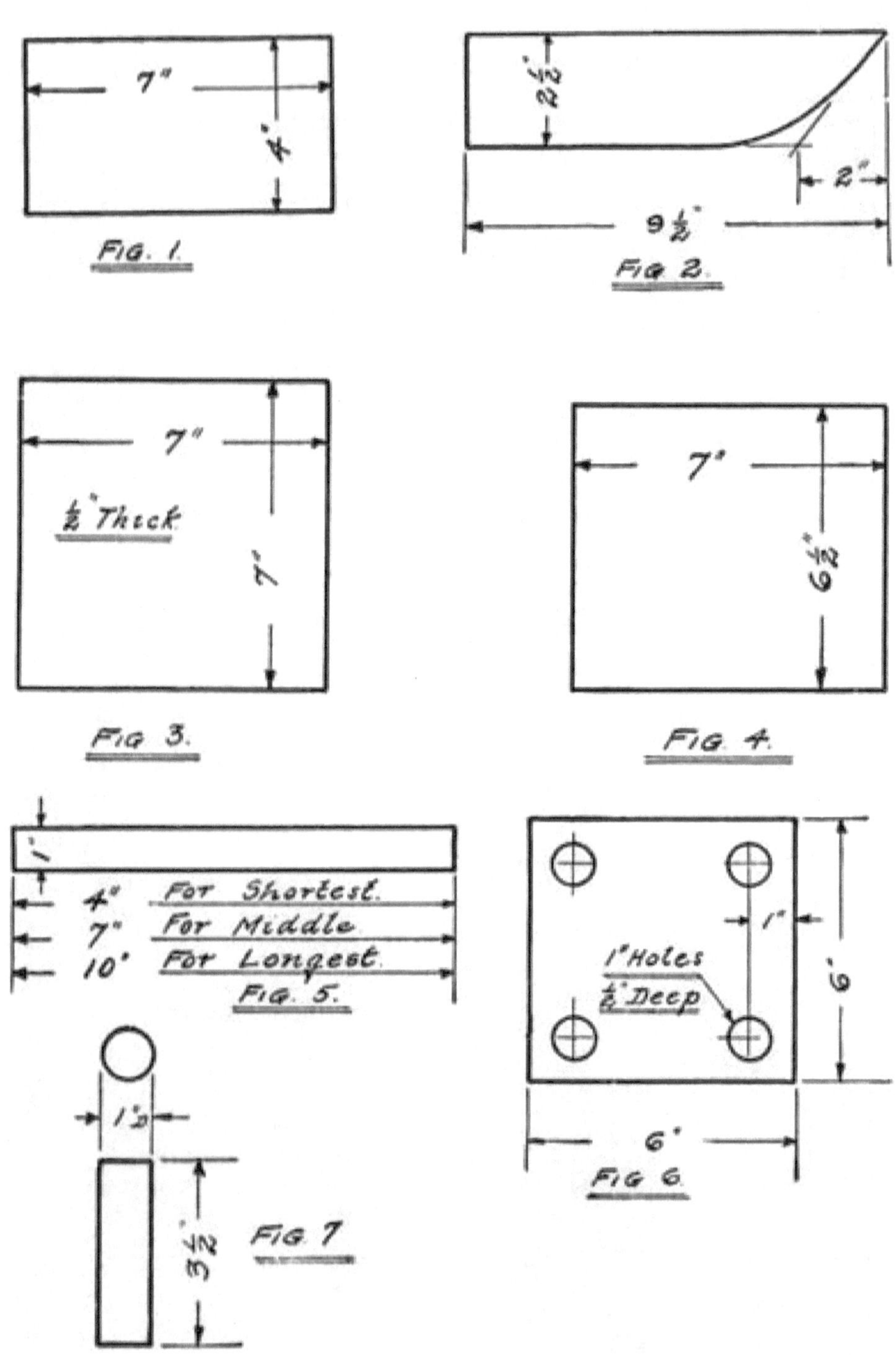

Diagrams of a Sled, a Chicken Coop and a Table.

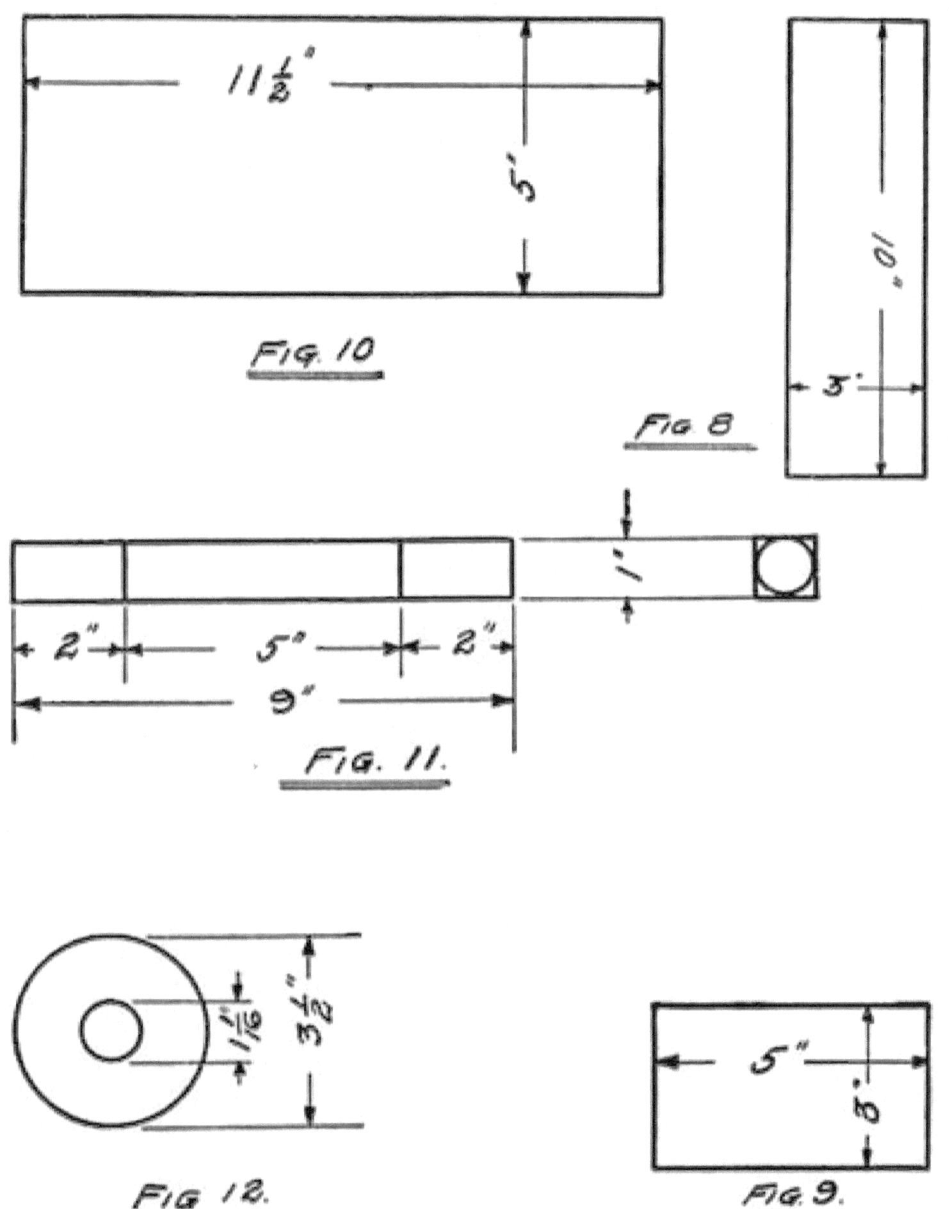

Diagrams of a Cart.

A little table may be made from one block of wood six inches square, and four cylinders three and a half inches long. For the table top (Fig. 6) select a piece of wood about an inch thick. Make this true, and smooth the top with sandpaper.

Then mark on the under side a square which is four inches on a side, and exactly an inch away from each side of the table top. At the corner of this inside square are to be made the holes for the table legs. For these holes you will have to use a bit and brace, and make the holes one inch in diameter and a half inch deep. If you haven't a bit and brace, you can, with a little more trouble, whittle out the holes. For the table legs (Fig. 7) take four pieces of wood one inch square and three and one-half inches long. By whittling off each long corner edge you can make these from square prisms into octagonal, or eight-sided prisms. Then keep shaving off these corner-edges until the prisms are so many-sided that they are practically round. Smooth them with sandpaper, and glue in place in the holes in the under side of the table top.

A strong little cart may be made almost as easily as these other wood toys. Cut from some pieces of wood three quarters of an inch thick, two side pieces (Fig. 8) measuring three inches by ten inches, two end pieces (Fig. 9) three inches by five inches, and one bottom piece (Fig. 10) five inches by eleven and a half inches. In the center of one of the end pieces make a nail hole for the string to go through. Nail the sides and ends together, lapping the end pieces over the ends of the side pieces. Then nail the bottom piece on. For the shafts of the wheels (Fig. 11) take two pieces of wood nine inches long and one inch square. For a space of two inches in from each end make the shafts cylindrical just as you did the table legs, leaving the center portion, which is five inches long, square. Nail these shafts to the bottom of the cart at points two and a half inches from each end. Next cut from 1 inch-thick wood four wheels (Fig. 12), three and a half inches in diameter. These may be cut out roughly with a saw, and worked down to the marked line with the knife. Then cut in the center of each of these wheels a hole about one and one-sixteenth inches in diameter—enough larger than the shaft so that the wheels will turn easily. Slip the wheels in place, and drive into the shaft from opposite sides, outside of each wheel, two small finishing nails. These are to keep the wheels in place, and must be driven in carefully so as not to split the shafts.

These are all attractive wood basket toys to make, and besides this, each one of them may be adapted, by enlarging, for some real use. The sled, with the addition of iron strips for runners, may be really used; or by using two sleds and an extra board fastened to both so that they will turn, it may be made into a "bob-sled" or "double." The chicken coop, enlarged, will comfortably accommodate the mother hen and her brood of chicks which are the beginning of every boy's first poultry venture. The little table may grow into a flower stand, and the cart, made larger and stronger, will rival any shop-bought express wagon for durability and comfort.

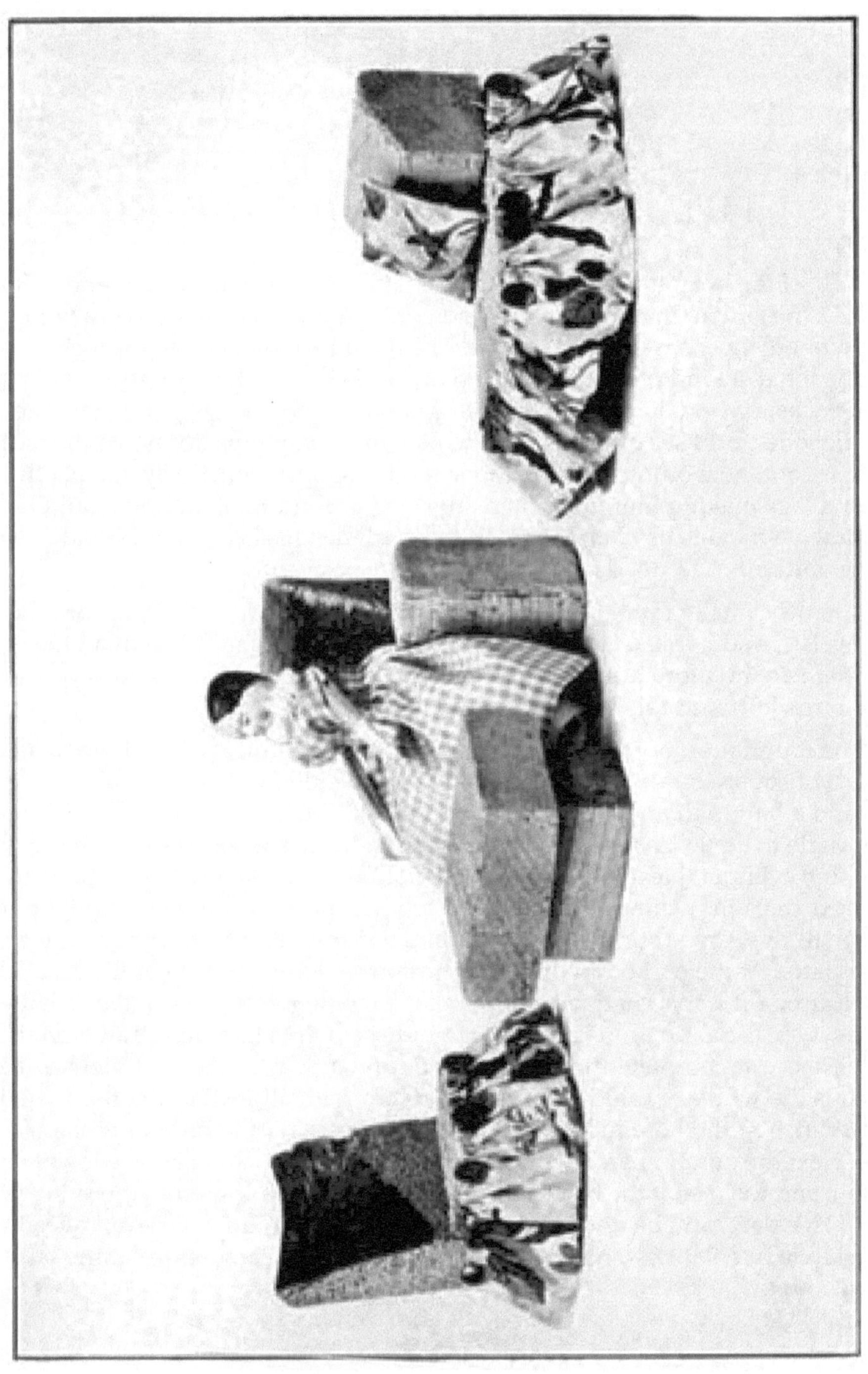

A Set of Dolls' Furniture Made by Glueing Together
Blocks of Kindling Wood.

THE WONDERFUL DODO BIRD

A VERY long, long time ago, in the far off country of Switzerland, which is the land of high mountains and goats and tourists, there was a wonderful bird. Nobody ever saw him near by, for he lived in a forest of alpenstocks, and he had the longest kind of legs, so that no matter how fast the tourists pulled up the alpenstocks, or how hard they tried to catch him, he always got away. The only way any one could see him was to watch the mountain tops, for when the weather was pleasant, he would climb up and stand there outlined clearly against the sky, his long legs making him taller than anything around him, and he would bob up and down—first his head and then his tail, and then his head again—and wave his plume and call, "Do-do, do-do."

The peasants made little dodo birds whittled out of wood, and sold them to the tourists, and because a real dodo bird was only hatched once in a blue moon, and there are no more blue moons, why, the ones the peasants made are the only dodo birds left. And this is how they made them.

The foundation of the bird's body (Fig. 1) is a chunky piece of wood an inch and a half square by three inches long. On each end of this is marked a circle—an inch and a half in diameter, which makes it just touch each edge. Then by cutting from circle to circle, as nearly straight as possible, the wood is made into a three-inch-high cylinder. Next one whole end is rounded off like the large end of an egg. The next steps in making the dodo bird are not quite as simple. A straight line is drawn all the way around the body, from end to end, which divides it into two equal parts. At the end of the line which represents the middle of the bird's back is measured off a space a quarter of an inch on either side. This makes a half-inch space which is the tip of his tail, and from these points lines are drawn on the flat end surface, to complete the four-sided figure shown in the end view of Fig. 1, which is the whole end of his tail. It tapers from a half inch at the top to about a quarter inch at the bottom, and when it is all finished, the bottom is slanted in a trifle. Next the bottom part is whittled up in a curve which meets the lower end of the tail, and the rest of the body is whittled in the shape shown in the side view of Fig. 1. This part can't be done by lines because it is a gradual curve all over. When this is done two flat slanting surfaces are whittled off for the sides of the tail.

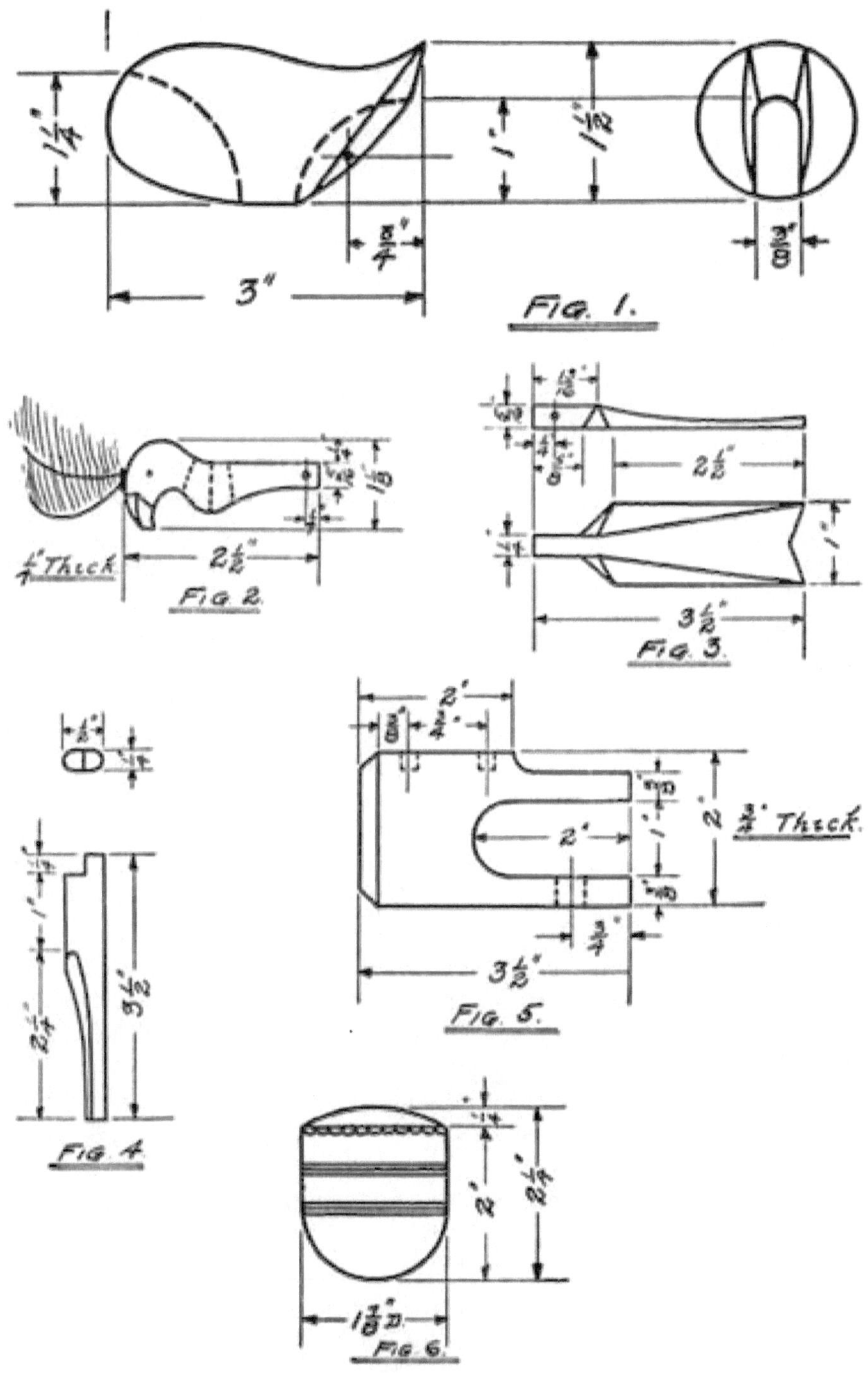

Diagrams of a Dodo Bird.

Now you are ready to make the grooves for the head and tail feathers to go in. Part of the lower center line has been whittled off and will have to be replaced. Then, measuring three-sixteenths of an inch on each side of this line, make parallel lines which shall extend around the lower part of the body from the end of the tail to a point on the front end just a quarter of an inch below the top. A space a half inch wide is left in the middle of the bottom for the legs to fasten on, and the rest is to be made into the grooves as shown on the pattern. The easiest way to do this is to cut as far in as possible, on the parallel lines which you have drawn, with a small saw. Then chip the wood out with a small chisel, and, with the chisel held bevel side down, round out the bottoms of the grooves. If you haven't such a chisel though, you can manage with a knife.

When the body is done, the rest is easier. Fig. 2 shows the head, made from a piece of wood two and a half inches long by one and one-eighth wide and a quarter inch thick. The outline is marked and whittled into shape, and the beak is slanted down to a point. One quarter of an inch from the end of the neck a hole is made for pivoting, the eyes are marked in with a pencil, and three rows of marks are made across the neck with a little pattern marking wheel. These may also be made around the body and will add to the beauty of the dodo bird. His plume is made of a soft, downy chicken feather, stuck into a hole in the top of his head and glued in place.

The tail feather (Fig. 3) is shaped like the feathered end of an arrow. The "feathered" part is one inch wide by two and a half long, and another inch in length forms the pivoting part. This end is a quarter inch wide and five-sixteenths thick, and the "feathers" are cut in from each side with a slanting cut as shown in the drawing. The bottom is left perfectly level, but the top is slanted down, with three flat cuts, to a sharp edge at the end. A hole is made from side to side, a quarter of an inch back from the small end, for pivoting. Two small nails driven through the body, with the head and tail feathers in position, form the pivots. They must be driven carefully so as not to split the wood, and must be placed so that the head and tail feathers will work up and down very freely.

The legs (Fig. 4) are pieces of wood three and a half inches long, a half inch wide, and a quarter of an inch thick. They are first whittled in an elliptical shape. Then the lower part, for a space of two and a quarter inches is tapered back from the front to give an appearance of standing very straight. At the upper end, for a quarter of an inch from the top, half of the wood is cut away, and the remaining part is fitted into holes cut in the body, three quarters of an inch apart, and glued.

The standard for the dodo (Fig. 5) is made like a small wooden vise. It is a flat piece of wood three and a half inches long by two inches wide and three quarters of an inch thick. One end is beveled slightly, and one end of the top is curved down slightly.

In the remaining flat surface on the top two holes are whittled out into which the dodo's feet are to be glued. Then a space two inches long and one inch wide is cut out to form the jaws of the vise. To tighten the vise there must be some sort of a screw through the lower jaw. A wooden thumb screw is not easy to get, so the best plan is to get a bolt about three eighths of an inch in diameter. Then cut a hole almost as large in your wood, and screw the bolt in, forcing it to cut its own "thread" in the soft wood.

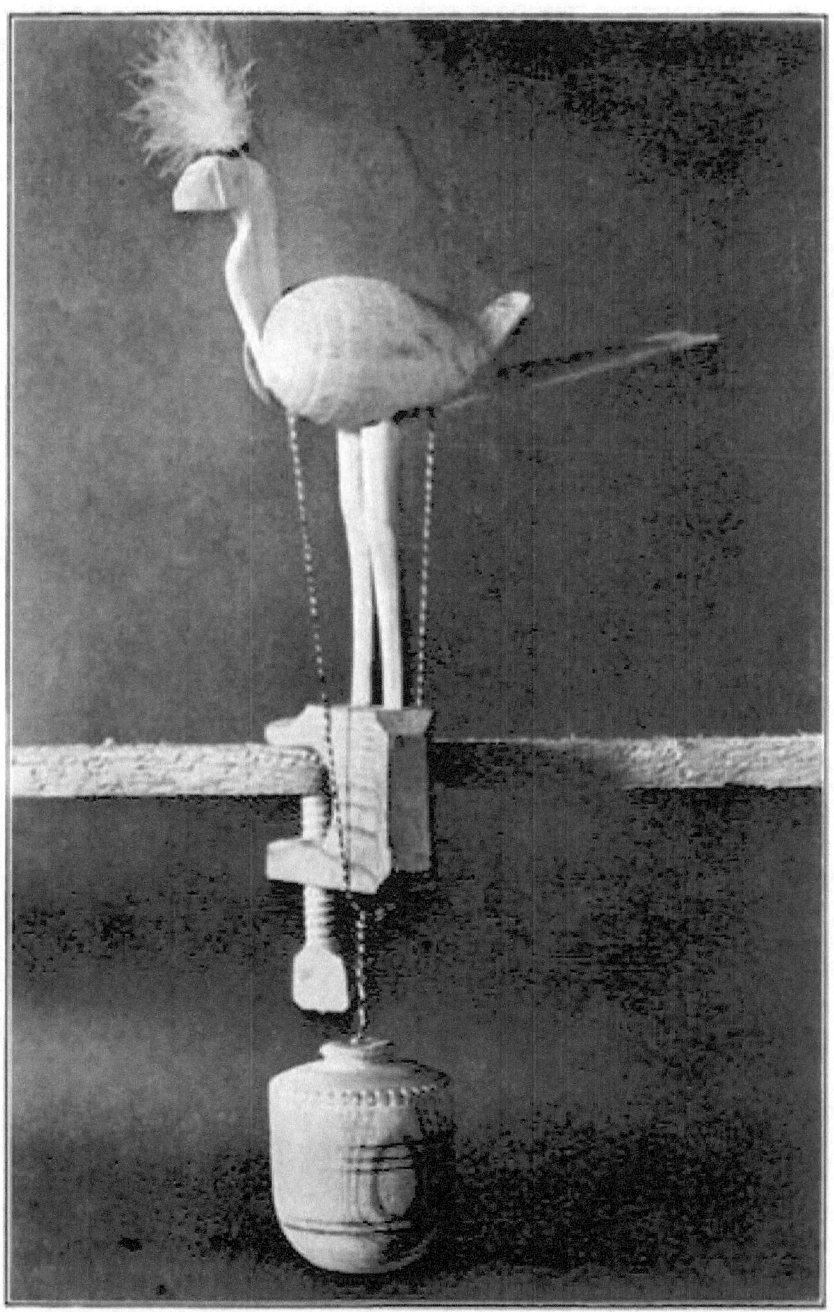

The Dodo Bird.

Fig. 6 is the weight which makes the dodo work. It is a piece of wood two and a quarter inches high by an inch and seven-eighths square. This is made into a cylinder and rounded at one end precisely as you did with the body. Then a circle is marked around it a quarter of an inch back from the flat end, and this end is slightly rounded off. It may be decorated or not, as you choose.

Now you are ready to make the dodo bird work. Take two pieces of string—stout, but not too heavy—about twelve inches long. Fasten an end of one of them—with a tiny wedge and some glue—into the end of the dodo's neck, and the other into the small end of the tail. Then bring the two pieces together and knot them about an inch from the other end. Fasten these two ends into the top of the weight just as you did the single ends.

Now fasten the vise securely on a shelf somewhere, and swing the weight to and fro like the pendulum of a clock. The dodo will bob first his head and then his tail and then his head again, and you can almost hear him calling "Do-do" way off on the mountain there. He's a source of never-ending fun, boys, and besides playing with him yourself, you can just watch and see how few grown-ups can go by him and resist swinging the pendulum.

A FLEET OF TOY BOATS

WHO remembers the mill pond down at the farm, clean, and high, with trees all about—a capital place for sailing boats? It is so small that, directly a toy ship is started on its voyage, you can run around the other side and meet her.

There is the trout brook, too, down in the woods, where everything is cool and still. There isn't a sound as you sit on the bank save when a mouse comes rustling along, pushing his way through the leaves with his queer little pointed nose, or a hedgehog plods by, blind and deaf, never seeing you at all.

If you should launch a toy boat in the brook, where do you suppose it would sail to? You will follow it a little way. Sometimes it will get caught in the ferns, or it may lie for a minute, stranded, on a rock, or it will overturn as it shoots the rapids. You start it on again with the long pole you cut from the willow tree, but presently the boat will sail away, out of a child's sight, down the brook.

Perhaps it will pick up a crew of little brownie sailor men. Perhaps it will stop somewhere to load a cargo of butterfly's gowns. You will lose sight of it though. That is what always happens to one's toy ships.

A boy can make himself a whole fleet of toy boats to play with in the mill pond and the trout brook. If one of them does go sailing away to Fairyland—why, what does it matter with all the rest of the fleet just tugging away at their ropes, waiting to be launched?

The little boats are the nicest of all, because one may have so many of them. Out in the woods there are some of last year's walnuts lying on the ground. Split one in half with a jack-knife, and take out all the meat, leaving the inside smooth and white. Glue a scrap of paper to a toothpick, and fasten this little mast to the inside of the half walnut shell with a drop of glue. There is a real fairy craft, fit for a dragon fly to ride in. Just watch it toss and float and sail away on the make-believe waves.

There are so many eggs in the barn, you can surely have one. Do you know how to blow an egg? Make a tiny hole with a pin in each end, then, by blowing steadily into one end, the contents of the egg may be emptied out of the other. You will be able to cut the egg shell lengthwise, now, with your jack-knife. If you have some paper strips you can bind the edges of the egg boat to make it a trifle stronger. Glue two paper seats across the top and add a pair of oars made of toothpicks. A tiny paper doll will enjoy a ride in the egg-shell boat.

A Cork Raft.

A Cork Sail Boat.

Out in the barn where you found the egg, there is a whole big bin full of corn cobs. Such light, clean playthings they are! They will make a stout little raft to float about in the mill pond. You will need to select eight corn cobs, all of the same size and length. Lay them side by side on the barn floor. Then split up an old berry basket, and cut two or more of the thin strips of wood from the side exactly as long as the raft is to be wide, lay these strips of wood across the corn cobs and nail them in place with tacks. The corn-cob raft is done. It is so light that it can be loaded with quite a cargo, two or three rubber dolls who do not mind the water, or a toy horse, or a rubber pig. Then, if the current is right, it will float way across the mill pond, and the toys can land on the other side.

Corks make a fine raft, too, and such a light one! A cork raft will almost never sink. You must collect corks for quite a while before you have enough for the raft. They will need to be of just the same width and length. Glue five or six corks together by their ends to form a little cork log. Make a number of these logs, and then fasten them together as you fastened the corn-cob raft. Another way of making the cork raft is to run the corks on a bit of fine wire and the logs may all be wired together in the same way.

A very large, flat cork, such as mother puts in her pickle jars, will make a fine little sail boat. All that it needs is a toothpick mast and a white cambric or paper sail glued on.

A paper row boat is very easy to make. Choose an oblong of heavy paper that will not soak with the water quickly. Fold a cocked soldier's hat. Every boy knows how to do that. Hold the cocked hat in the middle of each side and pull it out into a square. Bend back the two open sides to form another cocked hat, but smaller than the first one. Pull this out, also, into a square. Then, if you pull hard on the two closed corners, the paper will open into a fine little row boat. You can fold so many of these paper boats that a new one may be launched as fast as the old one sinks.

A boy who is clever with his jack-knife will be able to make a stout little sail boat from a piece of an old egg crate, or the side of a cigar box. The wood must be close grained and light—that is the first essential. Cut the boat, pointed at one end, and rub it smooth with a piece of sandpaper. Glue a meat skewer to the center for the mast, and hoist a little sail. A hole may be bored in the end of the sail boat, and a long string tied in will allow you to run along the edge of the brook and keep this little craft from sailing away.

There are other boats which will want to join this toyland fleet. Peanut shells may have very tiny paper sails pinned to the ends. A race between two rival peanut boats will be great fun.

A cigar box boat may have squares cut from the sides with a knife for oar locks; with meat skewer oars, it will make a very creditable scow, flat-bottomed, and perfectly safe for any doll to go clamming in.

Clam shells may have paper sails fastened on with glue, and any kind of flat shell loves to go sailing away by itself on the water.

A strong square of birch bark may be folded and cut rounding at the ends to resemble a canoe. The ends are then sewed with a needle threaded with strands of sweet grass or stout cotton, making a tiny Indian craft. If you wish the canoe to be perfectly water tight, it can be lined with waxed paper.

There will be fun for all summer long for the boy who makes and sails his own fleet of toy boats.

Whittled Toy Sail Boat.

HOW TO MAKE A PLAY TENT

HAVING a tent out in the garden or on the lawn during the summer vacation makes each long, happy day twice as long, and just twice as happy. A boy can play that he is an Indian, or a first settler, or a cave dweller, or even an old story book king if he has even the crudest kind of a roof over his head and some sort of a play shelter beneath which he can live and play, and dream all manner of delightful things.

Of course the nicest tent of all is one from a real tent factory made of canvas and having staples and pegs to fasten it to the ground, but such a tent costs ever so much money, and not every mother and father can afford to buy it. One family of children went without fireworks on Fourth of July that they might save the money which they would have, otherwise, burned up and with it they bought themselves a tent which lasted much longer than the smoke and noise of the fireworks would have.

There is, though, a very fine tent indeed, and one that will give a group of boys quite as much pleasure as any manufactured one. This is the home-made tent. It is the tent that seems to really belong to you because it is a sort of a makeshift and you make it with your own hands. There are ever so many ways of making your own tent, all of them simple and quite easy for one to follow.

One very strong and serviceable tent has a foundation of straight, young birch trees or saplings cut in the early spring and used for tent poles. Holes should be dug, and the poles set in the ground a quarter their length that no summer wind storm can uproot them. Around each pole, the earth is then pounded down, and the tops of the poles, six or eight in number, should be lashed together with cord. A couple of old army blankets may be stitched together to make a covering for this tent. A hole is cut in the center and the covering is slipped over the supports and tied to the base of each pole. There will be enough extra blanket to make a flap in the front of the tent to act as a door. If there is a summer shower when the children are playing in this blanket tent they may pull the flap tight shut, and just snuggle inside, listening to the raindrops that do not soak through the blanket covering one bit.

A second home-made tent has a foundation of bean poles or clothes poles for supports. These are sunk in the ground and fastened together at the top as were the saplings used for the blanket tent. The covering, however, is of brown denim. Twelve yards will make a very good-sized tent. The lengths are cut to fit the poles used as tent supports; they are pointed at the top, and stitched together. Tape sewed at the top, center, and base of each seam, on the inside, may be tied around the poles and fasten the covering to the props. This tent may be decorated in such a way that it will make a real patch of color on the lawn or in the back yard, and will have the appearance of an Indian's wigwam. Red and green, or yellow denim is used for the decorations. Small conventionalized trees, moons, stars, leaves, or any preferred designs are cut from the colored cloth and stitched to the brown covering. Another way of decorating the denim tent is to paint pictures on it with stencil colors, using stencil patterns of Indians, animals, or flowers. These colors are "fast" and the rain will not wash them off as is apt to happen in the case of designs applied with colored cloth.

A flower tent is a new sort of playhouse and is quite delightful in sunshiny weather. When it rains you can watch your tent grow from the house windows. It will be wise to select a fence corner, where a row of castor beans will sprout in a night almost to help form the back of the tent. Between these castor plants, there may be some quick-growing vine planted; mock orange, morning glory, or moon flower. As the seeds sprout and the vines begin to grow, they should be twined upon strings which extend up the fence and across the top between the two sides of the fence, forming the tent roof. Before summer is over, this roof will be a thick one as the vines increase their leaves and the leaves themselves grow larger and more lavish of their shade. After a while they will hang over the front of the tent helping to form a third side, and when the tent bursts into blossom the children who live inside it will feel almost as if they were in fairyland.

These tents all take time to make, but there are other home-made tents that can spring up in a day in the garden. A very little boy can set up grandfather's big green umbrella for a tent and have a pleasant time sitting under it. The handle can be buried a little way in the ground and there will be plenty of room beneath its delightful green shade for a boy and a picture book, or a little girl and her doll. To make this umbrella tent still more snug and sheltering, grandmother's shawl can be draped around it, or a rug may be pinned to the edges to form the back and walls.

Two boys who live next door to each other and are the friendliest of neighbors can make a tent that they can share. The village carpenter will furnish four stout pine posts a little taller than the fence between the boys' homes is high. Two of these posts are set up on one side of the fence about eight feet from the fence itself, and two on the other side in just the same position. The ticking cover of an old feather bed may be cut down to the right size, and nailed to the posts for a roof. A couple of old sails may be cut into straight curtains for the sides of the tent, with strips of lath in the hem so that they can be rolled up in pleasant weather. The tent is very cozy when it is finished, and before the summer is over nearly every boy in town will have been up to visit these boys in their little two-room tent.

HOW TO MAKE YOUR OWN TOPS

SOME toys don't know how to play. They just stand still and wait for a child to carry them around the garden or drag them by their strings across the nursery floor. They have no proper play spirit, these lazy toys, but that isn't the case with a top. Given a fair chance, just a fine, long string and a smooth side-walk—why, a top will play with a child all day long. It will twirl and whirl, never stopping to rest for long, and singing all the time its quaint little humming song to keep tune and time with its spinning.

You can buy a top for a penny at the toy shop, but it is just a plain, ordinary sort of wooden top exactly like all the other tops. How would you like to make your own tops? It will be the easiest task in the world to do this, and a whole lot of fun, too. The materials for home-made tops grow out of doors and are lying close at hand at home, in the wood-shed, or in the cellar.

Sharpen your jack-knife, and you may start out top hunting, at once.

A beet makes a queer little top that will spin gayly for a day, and if it breaks on the sidewalk or curbing, why you may pull up another top from the beet patch in the garden. The picture shows you a beet top that looks like a very own cousin to a wooden top because it is just the same shape, and the same size. There should be a pointed peg whittled from a scrap of soft kindling wood and stuck in the pointed end of the beet. The beet top is then wound with a string that has a small button mold or a little china button on the end and when you throw it as you do an ordinary wooden peg top, it will spin finely. A small turnip will make a top, too, if it has a whittled peg, and a little radish makes a fine top, save that it is too small to be wound up and should have a bit of toothpick stuck in opposite the peg to twirl it by.

The woods as well as the garden are full of tops. Let us go out top gathering under the nut trees some fine, frosty morning, taking the heroic little jack-knife, too, to help finish the tops. Fat acorns make splendid tops. A bit of twig should be whittled down to the right size and stuck in the flat end of the acorn by which to spin it. Every acorn has a fine point upon which to spin and a half dozen of these gay little acorn tops may be set spinning at once by a group of children in a top contest to see which will keep twirling longest. Horse chestnuts may be used for tops, too, if a child selects the very round, flat kind of nut. Horse chestnuts gathered when they first fall from the tree are soft and easily bored with an awl or darning needle, or the smallest blade of a jack-knife. A hole should be made exact-ly in the center of the nut and a perfectly straight piece of twig inserted, pointed at one end and extending a half inch above the horse chestnut at the top to hold it by.

Another way to make a horse chestnut top is to cut the nut in half, crosswise, and insert halves of toothpicks in each section, making two tops instead of one.

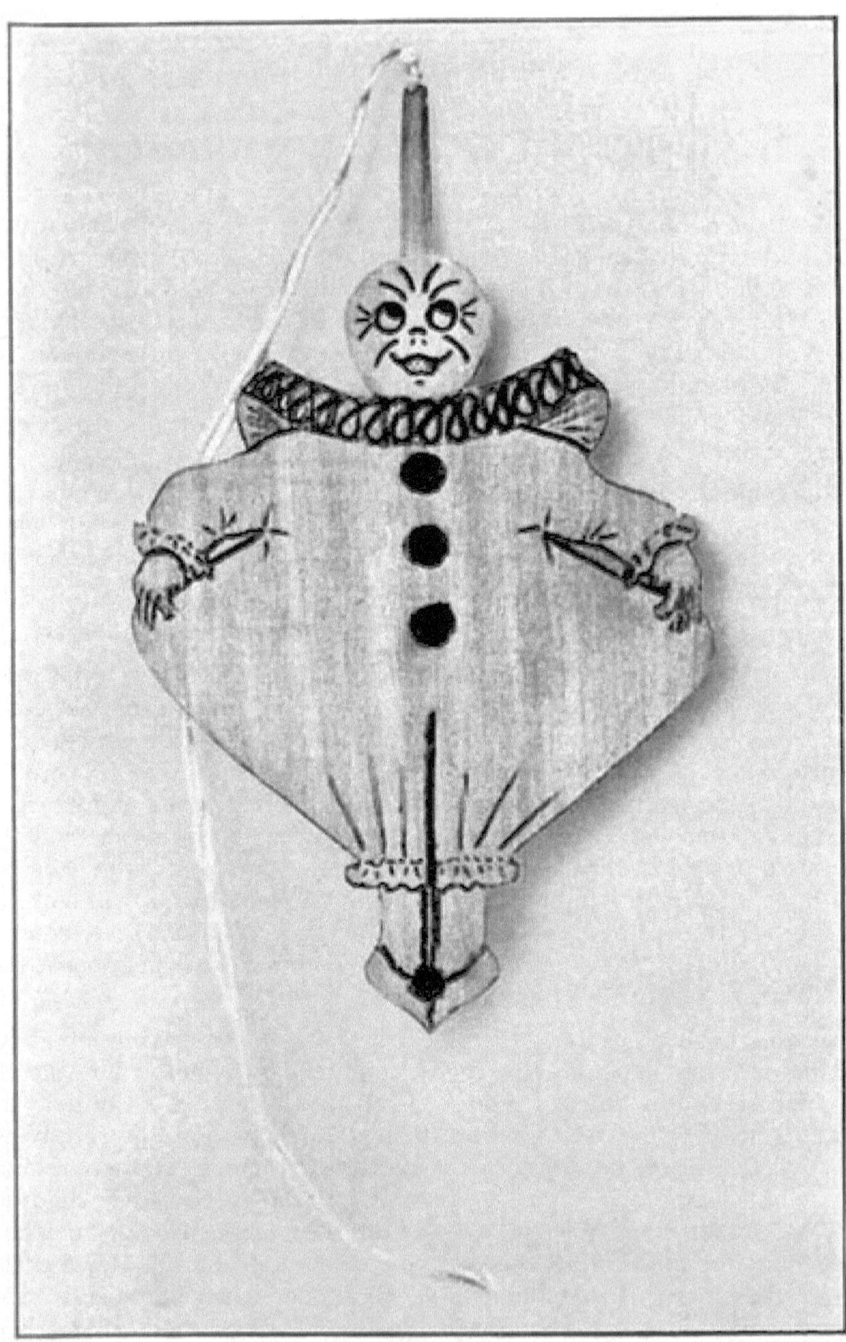

Whittled Clown Top.

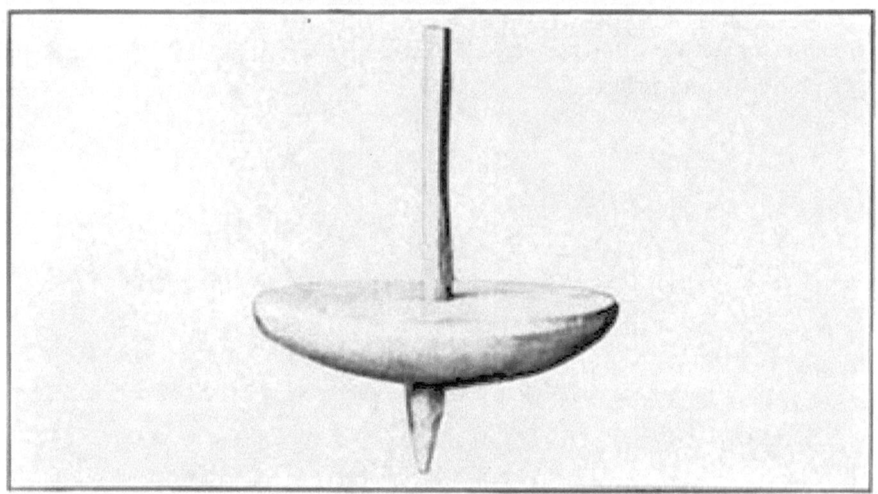

(A) Beet Top., (B) Top Made of Graduated Disks., (C) Button Mold Top.

When the shut-in days come in the winter and it is too late to pick your tops out in the garden or gather them in the woods, it will be ever so much fun to see how many tops you can make of the materials you are able to find at home. The wood that is used in a cigar box is soft and easily whittled, and just one box will furnish material for countless tops. The queer little circus clown in the picture spins on the tips of his toes if a top string is wound about the long peg protruding from the top of his head. He is not one bit difficult to make. The outline of a clown in a picture book is drawn on a sheet of tracing paper with a soft pencil and then transferred to a piece of the soft wood. If a boy has a jig saw it will be very easy to cut the little outlined clown in a jiffy, but it can be done in almost as short a time with a sharp jack-knife. When the clown is cut, his features are drawn in with charcoal or a soft pencil. If you spin him hard enough, he will rise right up off the ground once in a while and then settle down again and go on spinning. If a child has a book of brownies he can make a brownie top in the same way that the clown top was made. The brownie will spin on the tips of his little pointed toes.

The top in the picture that has a series of circles of different sizes will be ever so easy to make. The circles, each a half inch smaller than the one which is to be above it, are drawn on soft wood, and are then cut out with a jack-knife. A hole is cut in the center of each circle and they are fitted on a piece of wooden meat skewer, the point of the meat skewer forming the spinning end of the top. With a box of water color paints the circular disks of the tops are then painted in gay contrasting colors and the effect will be charming when the little top begins to spin.

Button molds make tops. The big wooden molds that the tailor uses for coats are best to make into tops. The hole in the center must be enlarged to admit of a sharpened end of a meat skewer being inserted. These button mold tops may be painted, too, and a splendid game can be played with them on the nursery table. Two stakes may be set up—the stakes from a parlor croquet set will do nicely—at the opposite ends of the table. The boys playing the game then choose colors and spin their button mold tops, whipping them with tiny whips made of meat skewers and colored twine, and trying to see whose top will make the distance between stakes first at the one spinning.

THE FARM THE SCISSORS BUILT

IT will be almost as fine as a real farm when it is finished and ever so much easier to make, because one will not need any boards, or tools, or huge nails to use in putting it together.

What do you suppose the barn is made of? Why, just a big piece of heavy wrapping paper that some one has brought to the house, and then has dropped on the hall table to be thrown away because it does not seem to be of any use now its wrapping days are over.

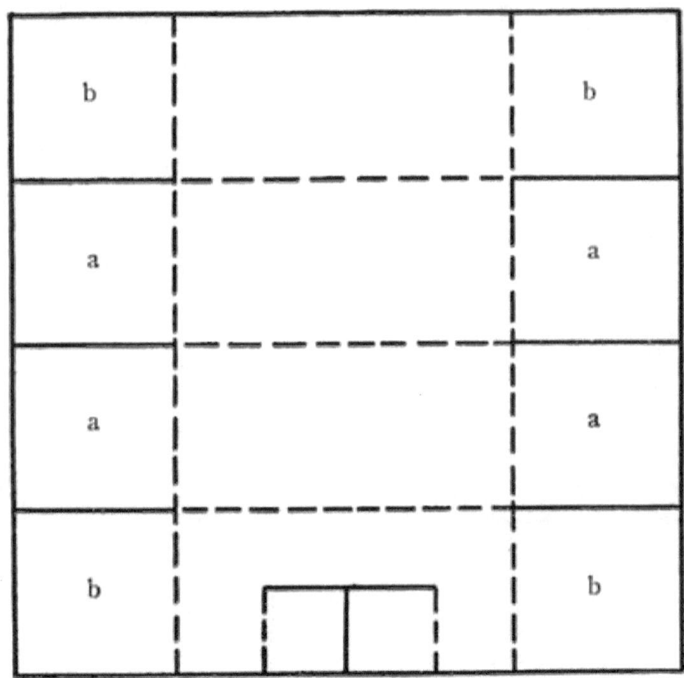

Folding for Barn.

First, one should cut the heavy wrapping paper into a large square. Then fold the square into sixteen small squares like the folding indicated in the diagram. Some of the lines in the diagram are dotted. Those show how the square is folded to make the little squares. Some of the lines are solid, heavy lines. Those are the lines to be cut. Make these cuts very carefully with scissors. There will be three cuts, each one square long and one square apart on two opposite sides of the paper. The two middle squares which are marked "a" in the diagram should be superimposed. That is a very, very long word, is it not? It means something very simple, though. These two squares are laid, one on top of the other, and are glued into place. Next, the squares marked "b" are brought together and their edges are glued. Then—one end of the wrapping paper barn is finished. Glue the squares at the other end of the barn in the same way, and cut a wide barn door. The door is made by cutting on a vertical crease on one side of the house, making two other cuts at right angles with the first one, and folding back the two sides of the door at the opening. If you want a window where you can toss hay up into the barn loft, it may be cut just above the door. A boy who has seen the inside of a real barn will be able to cut some strips of the heavy paper, and paste them together, fastening them to the back wall of the barn to show where the cow and the horse stalls are.

Some more strips of paper may be pasted together to form a barnyard fence. The barn may stand on the nursery table with the fence all around it, or an old suit box of mother's will make a very fine barnyard indeed. The sides of the box should be ruled with a pencil to look like the bars in a real barnyard fence. Then you can cut the bars with a jack-knife, or some sharp pointed scissors. When you have finished the suit-box barnyard, the barn may stand in one corner of it.

Now you are ready to cut some animals to live in the barn.

The pictures in your animal picture books will make splendid patterns for the barnyard animals. Trace the animals with some tissue paper and then transfer these patterns to some stiff paper. When you have cut carefully on the traced outline, you may paste the animal's feet to cardboard standards to make them stand up. There may be cows, and horses, and a donkey, and a whole flock of barnyard fowls. Then you may color the barn creatures with your water color paints or with colored pencils.

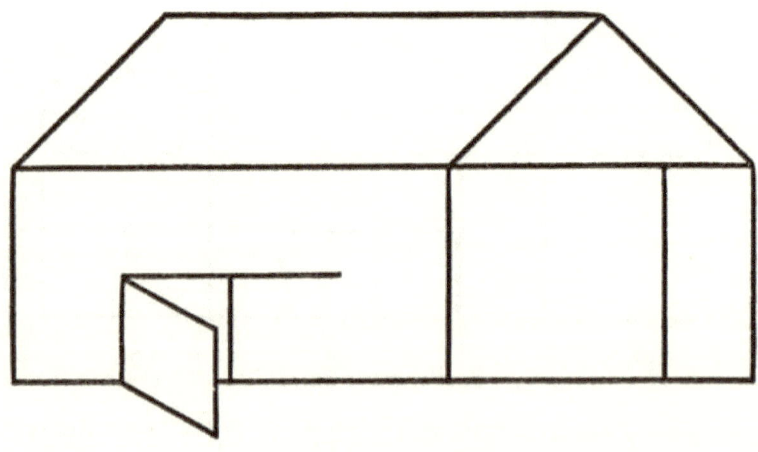

Finished Barn.

You can make a fine, large farm wagon, also, to stand beside the barn. To make the wagon, you should fold a small square of paper as you folded the large one for the barn. Instead of using the whole square, though, as you did for the barn, you must cut off a strip of four squares. Then make the short cuts as you did for the barn in the ends of the oblong piece of paper. Lay the three square laps which you have made by the cutting together, and paste them—one on top of the other. Cut out some wheels and fasten them to the cart. Glue on some cardboard or sticks for shafts, and the farm wagon is done.

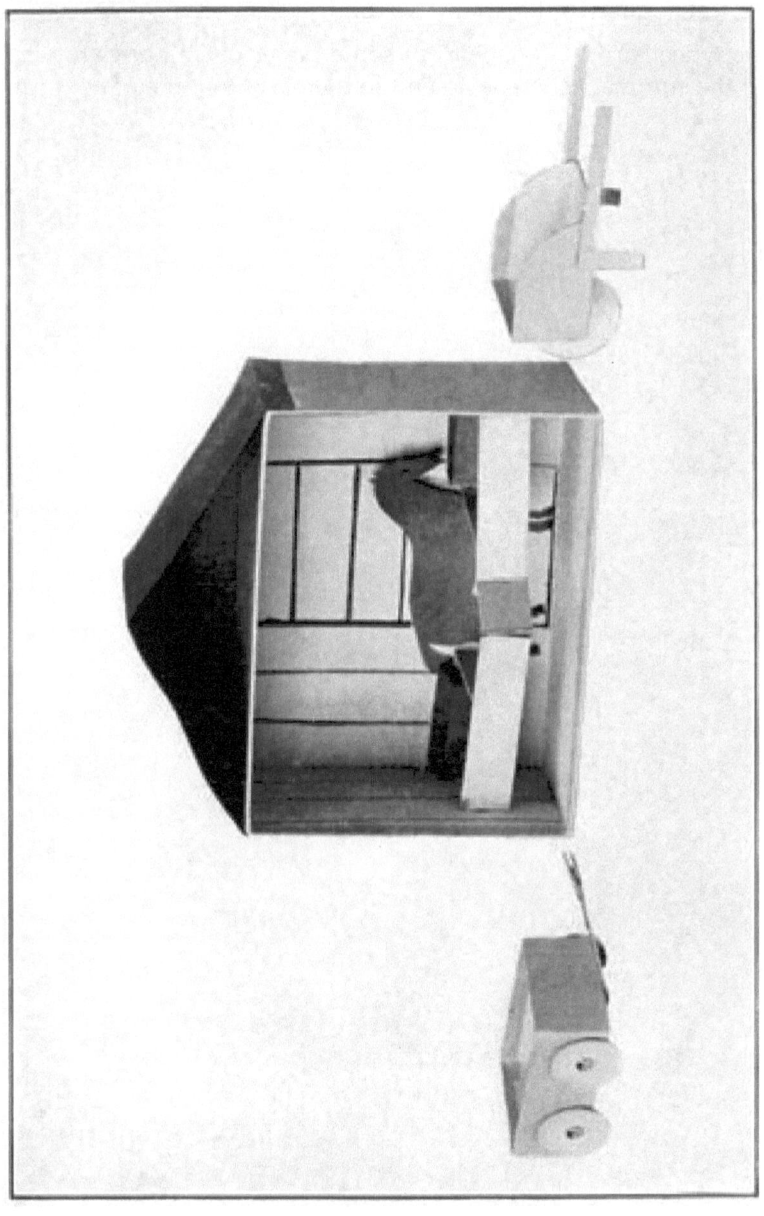

Cart, Barn and Barrow, Made of Cardboard Boxes.

If you want a wheelbarrow in the barnyard, you may cut one of mother's old spool boxes in half. The edges where you made the cut should be curved. A wheel made of an empty spool, or a cardboard disk may be fastened to one end with a pin, and some cardboard legs may be glued to the wheelbarrow.

When the paper farm is complete, you must harness the donkey to the wagon, and set him to work. Cut out some of the gay pictures of fruit and vegetables that fill the seed catalogues, and load the wagon.

Fill the wheelbarrow, too. Cut out some paper overall boys to visit the farm and spend the summer. There is no end to the plays that the paper farm will suggest to you.

MORE BOX PLAYS

ONE of father's empty note paper boxes, a starch box, a box that held spools of thread once—one, or all of these will furnish delightful play material for an afternoon in the house. A box has not finished its usefulness when its contents are gone. It is strong and tough often still, and ready for all kinds of fun.

Some cardboard boxes, large and small, will make the toy farm establishment shown in the picture. A box that once was filled with writing paper serves for the barn. The box stands on one side, leaving the entire front open that toy animals can be put in and taken out with greater ease than if there were a door. The long edge of the box cover is cut to fit the box, inserted and glued in place to form the front of the stalls which hold the toy animals. Shorter lengths of the cover edge are fitted in between the back of the box and this front partition to separate the stalls and are also glued in place. When these are in, a door can be cut. The stalls must be furnished with little grain boxes for the play horses to eat from; and this is the way to make them.

Measure with a school ruler and cut out a four-inch square of heavy wrapping paper. Lay the paper on a table in front of you and fold, first, the front edge up to the back, and then the front and back edges down to meet the center fold. Now turn the paper around, repeating the folding until there are sixteen squares. Cut off a row of four squares, leaving an oblong piece of paper that contains twelve squares. Make two cuts in the opposite narrow ends of the paper, one square long and one square apart. Fold up these squares and paste them, one on top of the other, forming a little oblong box. One of these boxes pasted to the back of each stall looks just like a grain trough, and may be filled with oats, if a country boy is making the farm, for the little horse to eat.

Some of the wrapping paper that remains after the grain boxes are finished makes the roof of the barn. Cut a strip as wide as the barn is deep and once and a half as long. Fold it once through the center and, at the ends, fold down flaps by means of which the roof can be glued to the top of the box forming a hay loft. When spring comes you can cut grass blades with a pair of gardener's shears, dry them in the sun, and fill the loft of this little box barn with real, play hay.

A box in which the apothecary packs his powders makes the little farm cart in the picture, and another one the wheelbarrow. No cutting is necessary for the cart, but some of the cardboard left in the cover of the note paper box can be used for wheels. A fifty-cent bit is the right size for the wheels. Lay one on the cardboard, and draw carefully around it with a pencil, cutting four of these wheels with a pair of sharp scissors. Brass paper fasteners will make strong hubs for the little wheels.

Pierce a hole through both wheel and box before inserting the fastener, though, to help the wheel to turn. A strip of the box cover glued to the front of the cart serves for the handle.

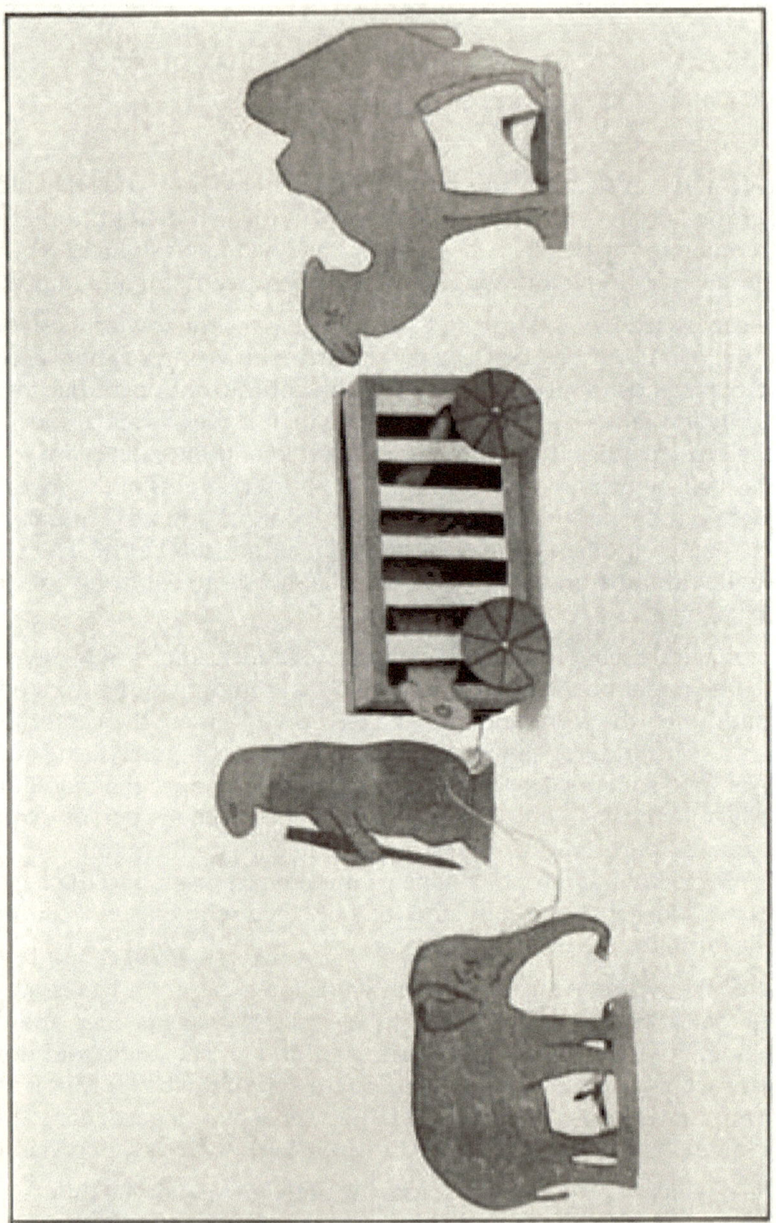

Circus Parade (The Cage is Made of a Shoe Box).

The wheelbarrow is just a little more difficult to make than these other toys, but not too great a task for a child with clever fingers. A section that is about one third of the entire length is measured and cut off the second small box, and thrown away. It is the remaining two-thirds of the box that is to make the wheelbarrow. The front, open edges of the box are now curved like the sides of a real wheelbarrow. Two narrow strips of the cover, or two small sticks are glued to the front of the wheelbarrow for handles, and two shorter lengths of cardboard or two very tiny sticks form the legs. Another cardboard circle cut the same size as those used for the cart wheels is inserted by means of a knife cut in the back of the barrow and helps it to trundle along.

The box-built cart and wheelbarrow will be found most useful in the spring. They can be loaded with little green apples, tiny brown pebbles that look like toy potatoes, corn kernels, or peas. They will be strong enough to last a whole season and help to carry fodder to the horse who lives in the box barn.

There is still more box fun. Ask mother for an empty cardboard starch box, the strong kind covered with blue paper, and see what a fine little toy garage it will make. Almost every child has a toy automobile given him for Christmas, but it is so apt to go steering away with its own gasoline, and losing itself somewhere in the house if a child has no special place in which to keep it.

Take the cover of the box and turn the box itself bottom side up. On one side, right in the center, draw a big square. The lower part of the square should come on the very outside edge of the box because this square is to be the garage door. The door should be made in two parts, so as to open very wide and admit the automobile when it comes steaming along in a great hurry. To make this double door, draw a perpendicular line that divides the square into two parts. Then, with a pair of sharp scissors cut right up this line to the top of the square. Next, cut along the top line to the right and left of the middle line. Folding back the two halves that have just been cut, out toward the outside of the box, makes two little doors and opens the front of the garage. Square windows can be cut in the sides of the box, as many as one wishes.

A number of empty thread boxes will make a splendid train of cars, strong enough to drag a whole family of china dolls or a load of live stock up and down the piazza or along the garden path. Cardboard circles cut from the covers of the thread boxes and of the same size as those used for the wheels of the toy cart make the car wheels. They are fastened on, either in similar fashion to the cart wheels by means of paper fasteners, or a bone collar button may be pushed through cart and wheel, helping the wheels to revolve more easily. One of the thread boxes has the cover glued on, and to the top is glued also one large wooden spool for the engine's smoke stack, and a block for the engineer's cab. These little box cars are coupled together by short lengths of braided cord. Holes are punched in the ends of the cars with an awl and the cord is pushed through and knotted at each end to hold it in place. A long piece of cord is fastened to the engine and is used to draw the cars by.

There is no end to the entertainment and fun to be had from a pile of empty boxes. Just get to work at a few of them your next free afternoon and find out how much they are able to help you in your play.

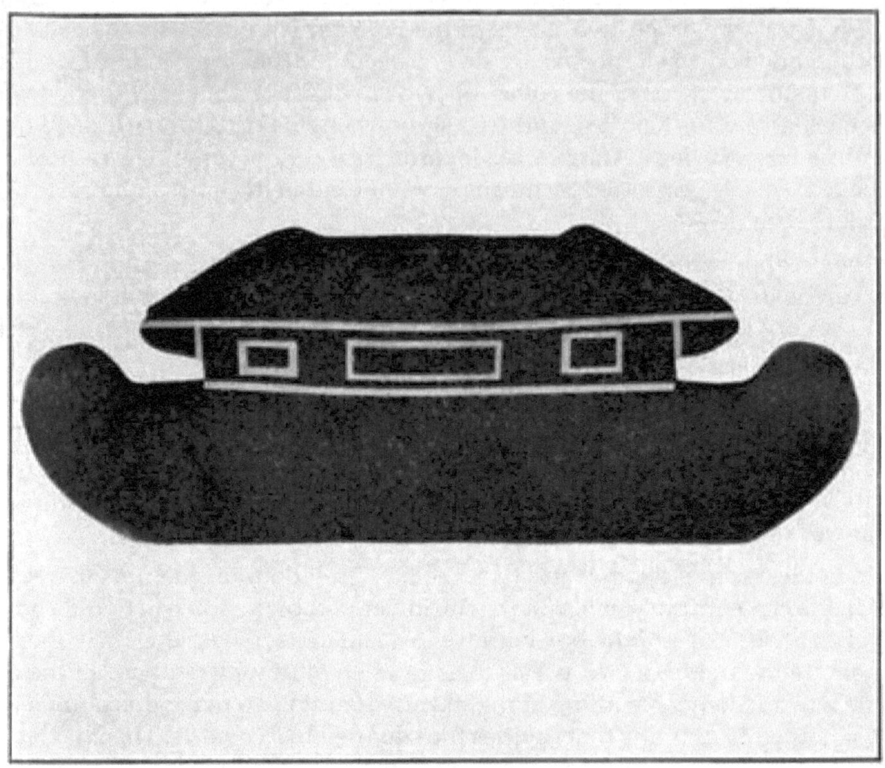

(A) The Ark, (B) Cardboard Animals Who Live in the Ark.

A RECIPE FOR A NOAH'S ARK

IT isn't a very difficult recipe to follow. All the stirring you need to do will be when you mix up some flour and a little water to make the paste. That is the first ingredient. Next in the recipe comes a pair of sharp scissors and a pencil. After that you must find some sheets of heavy paper, and the old animal picture books that you thought you could not enjoy any longer because the leaves were coming apart and the pictures were torn. Spread out all these things on the nursery table, and you will be ready to begin the Noah's Ark.

The Ark itself is to be a big, strong envelope for holding all the wild animals, and this is how you must make it. One of the sheets of heavy paper should be folded in half. The folded edge forms the bottom of the envelope. Beginning with this folded edge, the outline of the Ark is drawn on the paper with your pencil. It is a simple outline to draw—a big boat with curved ends, and a sort of house resting on the top. Then, holding the folded edge tightly so that the paper will not slip, cut out the Ark. The ends of the Ark should be bound or glued, but the top is left open that the animals may be put in.

Windows and a door are cut in the Ark for the animals will want to look out as they sail away on their wonderful voyage, and the Ark may be painted bright red with green trimmings.

Next come the animals.

The pictures of the animals may be mounted on one of the remaining sheets of heavy paper, so they will be stiff enough to stand up alone. That is one way of making enough animals to fill the Ark, but there is another way that will take a little longer, but will prove ever so much more fun.

The loose pictures from the book of animals should be fastened to the table with thumb tacks, or tacked to a drawing board. A square of white tissue paper is then laid over each, and the outline of the animal's body is traced with a soft pencil. When the tracing is finished, the tissue paper is carefully lifted off and laid with the plain side up on some stiff white cardboard. The outline is then retraced with the same soft pencil leaving a pattern of the animal on the cardboard. The animal is then cut out, and painted with the nursery water colors.

You will need to be very clever, indeed, to paint the animals so that they will look as if they were just fresh from the jungle. There must be a tawny lion colored with brown that has a great deal of yellow ocher mixed with it. The panther must be orange with big yellow spots, and large green eyes. The tiger's eyes must have yellow mixed with the green paint and his coat is yellow with orange stripes. The bear is brown and the kangaroo is tan.

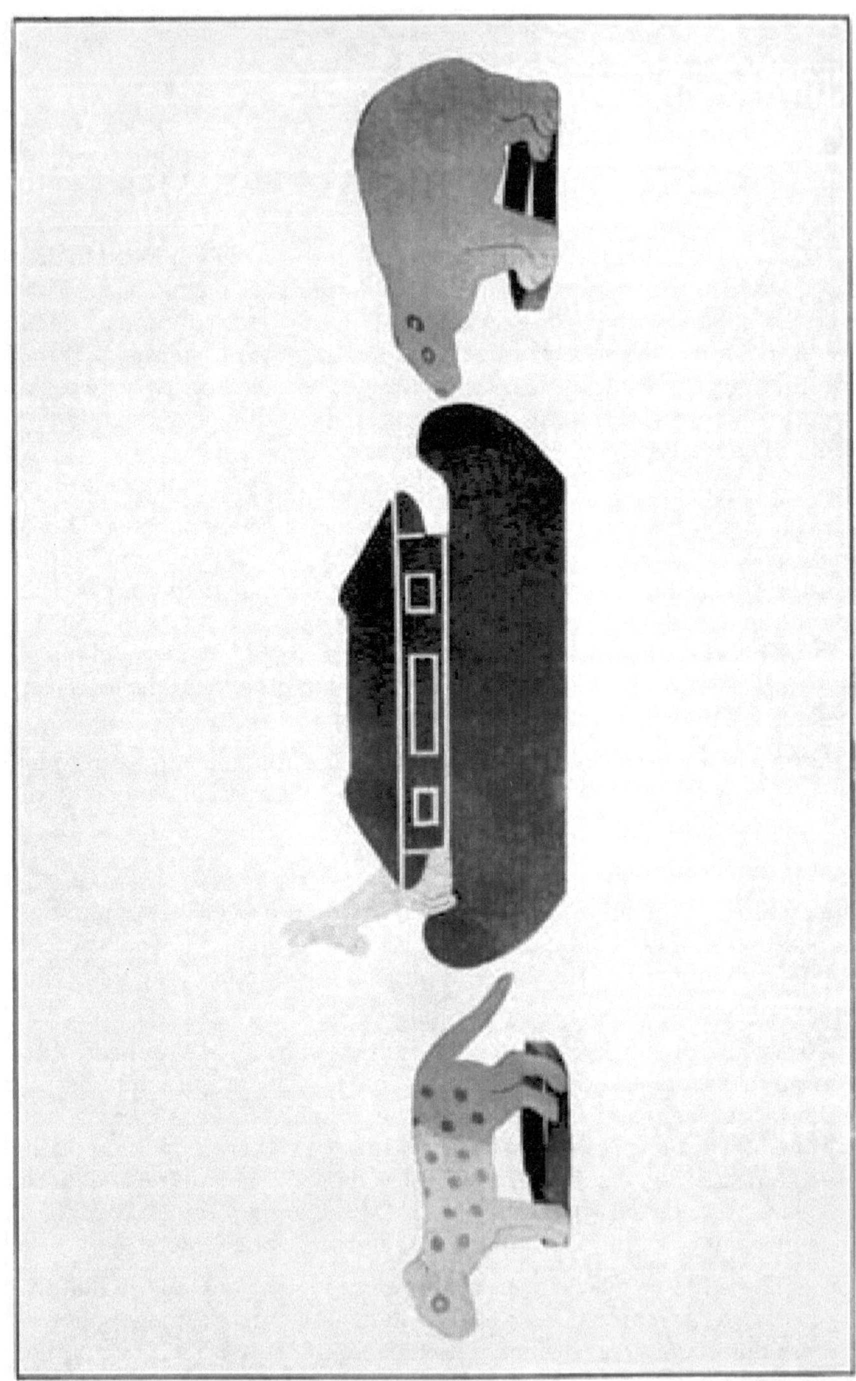

Going Aboard the Ark.

There should be two of each kind of animal. Now how shall you make them stand up and walk like real, live animals? Some very tiny bits of wood may be glued to their feet. That is one way of making the animals stand. Another way is to make a narrow ring of the same cardboard from which the animals were cut. The animals' feet are then glued to this ring, and they will really stand.

A boy will be able to make more animals than he can count,—leopards, monkeys, zebras, elephants, as many as he can find patterns for in his toy picture books. And it will prove such fun to draw them and paint them that he will be kept busy for many rainy afternoons.

HOW TO MAKE YOUR OWN UNIFORM

EVERY boy needs to be a soldier, once in a while. There are so many brave deeds to be done and so many cowardly things to fight, and so much dark to walk through courageously, and so many strange dogs and cats, and shy little girls to protect with all the gallantry of those old, old knights who lived in the story-book days. A soldier boy is never late for school, and he never, never forgets to do an errand. He goes to bed alone every evening at eight, even if the stairway is dark, and there is no light in the upstairs hall to chase away the ghosts. He never lies, and he is always cheerful. He knows that being brave and gallant and true is just as much a part of a soldier's duty as marching, and drumming, and saluting Old Glory.

It isn't easy to be a soldier though in a plain, everyday suit of clothes, made of homespun perhaps, and patched, and dingy brown in color. A real soldier suit cut and fitted the right size for a boy costs more money than there is in the boy's tin bank. What is the boy going to do if he wants more than anything else to be a soldier and he hasn't enough money to buy himself a suit?

Any boy will be able to make the soldier trappings shown in the picture, and when he puts on the cap, and the shield, pins the epaulets to his shoulders and sticks the play sword in his belt, he will be ready for the life of a little soldier. He can work or play cheerfully, and when it comes Saturday, or Washington's Birthday, he will be the envy of all the other boys as he leads them in a fine parade, dressed in his gay, home-made soldier things.

Suppose we make the soldier's cap first. The diagram marked Fig. 1, 2, 3, and 4, shows just how to do the construction. A bright red cap will be fine for the soldier, or a blue one just the color of the blue field in the flag. There is a kind of tough, half-heavy paper called book cover paper. One can order it from a stationer's shop or a printing factory at a cent or two a sheet. Some sheets of this will make the boy's own cap and enough for all the other soldiers in the regiment. A piece of paper that measures fourteen by twenty inches is the foundation for the soldier cap. Fold the two narrower edges together until they touch, and crease the paper through the center as shown in Fig. 1. Then with the paper still folded, make a second fold as shown by the line in Fig. 2. This line forms a guide line for the next two folds which make the point of the cap. Lay the papers, open, as in Fig. 1, on a table with the folded edge at the back; fold each half of the back edge down along the line made by the last folding. Then fold up and crease the lower open edges forming the rim of the cap. The rim should be glued down to make the cap firm and strong. A feather can be made by fringing strips of red or blue crépe paper and twisting them around a narrow strip of cardboard which is glued inside the rim of the cap. A turkey's feather will do just as well, or a bunch of hen's feathers, or a cockade made of red, white, and blue ribbons to decorate the cap.

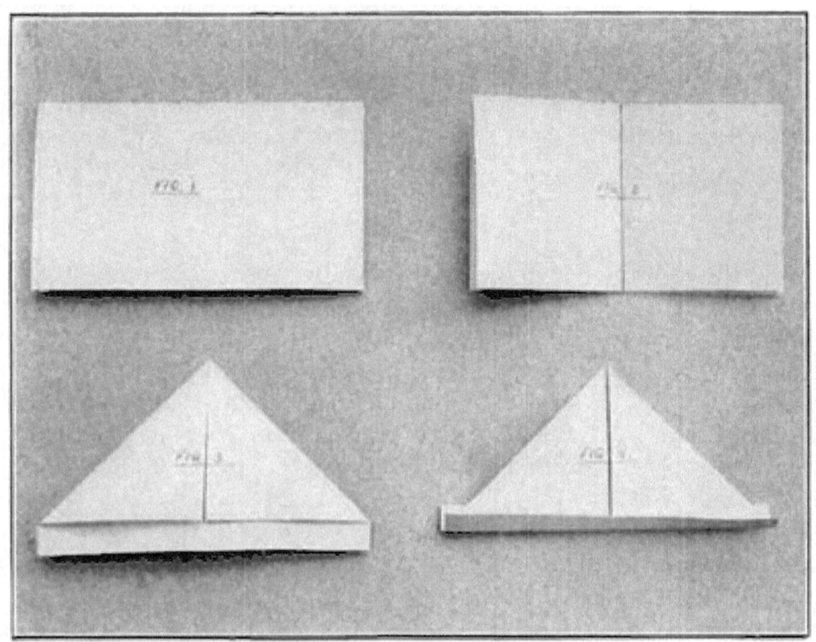

(A) Pattern for Soldier's Cap, (B) The Finished Uniform: Cap, Shield, Sword and Epaulets.

A boy can find a splendid shield pattern in the back of the dictionary. Copy it, and enlarge it until it is the right size to cover a boy's shirt bosom. Then draw it on heavy white cardboard, and cut it out. A good size for the shield will be eight by ten inches. When it is cut it can be decorated with stars and stripes with colored pencils or paints as shown in the picture. The stripes are drawn carefully with a ruler and filled in with color; one red and one white. The blue ground above the stripes is dotted with stars cut from gilt paper and pasted on. Two holes are punched in the sides of the shield, and a bit of cord is strung in by means of which the shield may be hung around a boy's neck. It will make his heart beat faster and give him a whole lot of courage every time he looks down at its brave stars and stripes.

Now for the sword which looks like a formidable weapon in the picture, but is really not dangerous at all. Every boy knows how to roll a narrow piece of paper, and make a lamp lighter. The sword that is part of this home-made soldier suit is made in just the same way. Cut some narrow strips of the book cover paper and join them with glue until there is a long strip. Roll this strip of paper tightly, in lamp lighter fashion, until it is fifteen inches long. Then press it flat between heavy weights. Roll a second strip of paper for a length of six inches and glue it to the broad end of the sword as a handle. These swords are so delightfully easy to make that a boy will want to roll a dozen after he has made his first one, and he can arm himself with as many paper poniards as an Indian chief has arrows in his quiver.

The soldier's epaulets are just five by two inch strips of the book cover paper cut to fit a boy's shoulders and decorated with fringed red and blue tissue paper. They can be pinned to the soldier's coat shoulders with safety pins and will make an ordinary play suit quite as military in appearance as any uniform.

When the boy soldier is dressed in this home-made uniform, which will be even more effective than any which is for sale in a toy shop, he will be ready for any adventure in addition to the brave prowess of everyday life. Perhaps he and the other boys will want to take one of mother's old blankets and two or three clothes poles for a tent, and tramp as far as the woods for a day of real scouting. Every soldier has a knapsack for carrying provisions and this play soldier will need one, too. A large, flat box makes a fine knapsack. Inside can be packed a bundle of sandwiches, two or three apples, a doughnut or two, and a piece of pie or a big slice of pound cake. When the box is packed, tie it securely with a length of cord, and have one end of the cord for a strap by means of which the knapsack is hung across the soldier's back. Roll a square of old blanket and tie to the top of the box just as a real soldier fastens his blanket to his knapsack, and the make-believe soldier in cap, epaulets, and shield can draw his sword and start off in search of any adventure.

JOINTED TOY ANIMALS.
HOW TO MAKE THEM

THEY will really do "stunts," these toys in the picture. The grasshopper will hop if you stand him up on a table and give him a chance. The turtle will crawl along much faster than an ordinary, live turtle. The crocodile will follow you so fast that you will surely be eaten by him unless you hurry. What fun it is going to be to play with these live toys, but first a child must make them, and as many more as he likes.

Clear a low table on which to work and find some heavy cardboard or thick water color paper from which to construct the animals. Bring also, a pair of strong scissors, a sheet of tracing paper, a soft lead pencil and the box of water color paints you found in your stocking last Christmas. These are all the tools and material necessary for making a barnful of animals. Ask mother for some porcelain collar buttons to fasten the animals' legs to the bodies. The laundry man brings so many of these useless studs every week and a crop of them will be fine for jointing the animals. If one cannot find enough collar buttons, a box of tiny brass paper fasteners will serve very well instead.

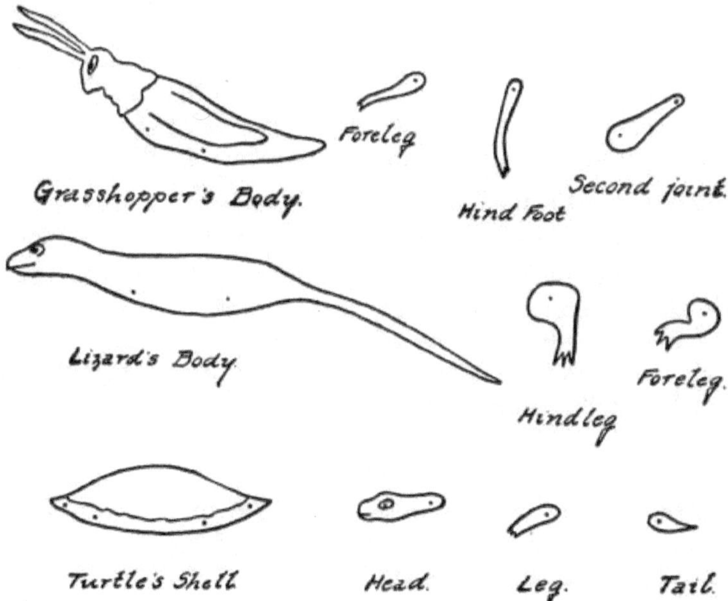

Every boy knows how to draw a few animals, at least free hand. If he is clever enough to be able to do this just by watching the horses out in the street, or the tiger in the Zoo, or the kitten who sits in front of the nursery fire, washing her face, so much the better. He will not need any patterns. The child who finds difficulty in sketching an animal free hand will have to trace his patterns from a book, or a toy animal. Often one of the nursery toy animals may be laid flat on the cardboard and its outline drawn and cut. Noah's Ark animals, if they are large, make excellent patterns for a child to copy. If one has no toys of the right size, the tracing paper may be laid over the picture of an animal in a farm picture book, or a book that tells about the jungle, or a book on Natural History. When the outline of the animal has been neatly traced on the tracing cloth, it should be transferred to the cardboard from which the animal is to be made. When a child has obtained a clear outline in this way, he may next proceed to make the animals alive.

First, he must decide just the location of the animal's joints. Where are the tiger's paws fastened to his legs? Where are the grasshopper's knees? Where, hidden underneath his shell are the turtle's funny little flat feet attached to his body? Then, using the pattern which has just been made, a new pattern of the creature's body is made, then a pattern of a leg, a tail, an ear, and these sections are all cut from the cardboard, separately, with scissors or the sharp jack-knife. In cutting out legs and paws, they should be made always a little longer than the original pattern to allow for the joint by which they are fastened to the body. As soon as all the parts of an animal have been cut from the cardboard, they should be laid in place and holes punched with a coarse needle or an awl at the joints. If the animal is a huge one, the collar buttons may be slipped in these holes to hold the sections together. In the case of the toy creatures shown in the picture, paper fasteners were used. When these joints have been made the toys will stand or sit, cock their ears or wag their tails, leap or run — in fact they will do anything a boy wishes.

The paints come next. It will be great fun to make the toy animals just the right color. A tiger may be such a gorgeous yellow with bright green eyes and black stripes. The grasshopper may be either green or a warm brown, and the turtle's house which he must always carry around on his back should be painted gray.

These jointed animals may be persuaded to act out the children's favorite stories and will furnish a new kind of fun for rainy afternoons in the house.

Little Brer Rabbit can be easily made of white cardboard from the pictures of Peter Rabbit or the rabbit pictures on an Easter card. Then Brer Rabbit and Old Man Terrapin may act out on the nursery table the famous race that Uncle Remus has told us about. A shoe box may be used for a miniature stage if it is placed on its side on a table, some scenery is painted in at the back and a little cloth curtain hung at the front. Through a hole in one end the jointed animals may be put in and they will perform most acceptably for an audience of dolls.

Two children playing together, or two groups of children can each make a set of jointed animals and then pose them to illustrate a favorite story, the other child or group guessing the story illustrated.

Many other plays will suggest themselves when one has a set of animals which are really alive and which a child has made, all himself.

Jointed Cardboard Animals.

YOUR OWN CIRCUS

IT is going to be a circus small enough to fit in any house. In fact, it will be possible to put it within the boundaries of an old table. Because you can't always have an outdoor show is just the reason that you are going to plan this fine, diminutive one in the house. It may take several days to get it ready, but once your indoor circus is finished, you will find it almost if not quite as interesting as a real one.

First, find an old table somewhere to be used as a circus ground. A pine table will serve nicely, and if you can find some old green muslin with which to cover it, you will discover that it looks exactly like the grass in the field where the real circus is held. Tack the muslin to the under side of the table top so that it will not wrinkle and interfere with the circus parade. Now you are ready for the rope fence which always encloses a circus ground.

In the four corners of the table bore, with a gimlet, through the canvas, some holes that are just the right size to hold dowel sticks, five inches long. You can buy these dowel sticks of a carpenter in foot lengths at a few cents each. Glue the posts in the holes which you have bored in the table and also bore extra holes for two more about a foot apart in the front of the table. These last little posts are for the gate to your circus ground. When the glue has set and the posts are perfectly dry, tie cord to one, near the top, and then stretch it to another, knotting it, until you have finished the rope fence that encloses the circus ground. If you like you can have two or three rows of cord, and you can print a little circus sign to pin to the gate. It may read:

THE GREAT AND ONLY ANIMAL SHOW

Clowns, Wild Beasts, and the Biggest Elephant in the World.

Performances Every Afternoon and Evening.

Admission, Adults, two pins, Children, alone, one pin.

COME ONE. COME ALL!

All around the edges of the bill you can draw pictures of wild animals with your colored pencils.

The circus ground will look very much pleasanter if you have a few trees standing about on the edges, and these trees will be useful, also, to tie some of your wild beasts to.

Meat skewers will do nicely for the tree trunks if you fringe ever so many narrow, doubled strips of green tissue paper, and wind them with it, fastening the fringes to the meat skewer with mucilage. The green paper flutters in the air quite like real foliage in the breeze on circus day, and the little trees will stand up nicely if you stick the end of each skewer inside an empty spool, glueing it there so that it will stay in place.

Did you think that you were never coming to the tent for your circus? Well, here it is, and the picture shows you just how to construct it. You will need to enlarge the diagram several times the size which you see in the picture, but that is easily accomplished by means of your ruler and lead pencil. Use some sort of tough, firm paper for the tent. Water color paper will be splendid because you can get out your paint box and paint pictures of wild men and palm trees and animals on the sides. If you have no water color paper, use brown bristol board. The latter makes a fine stiff tent. Cut out the top and sides as carefully as you can, bend them, and glue or paste them together. Then stand the tent up in the center of your circus ground.

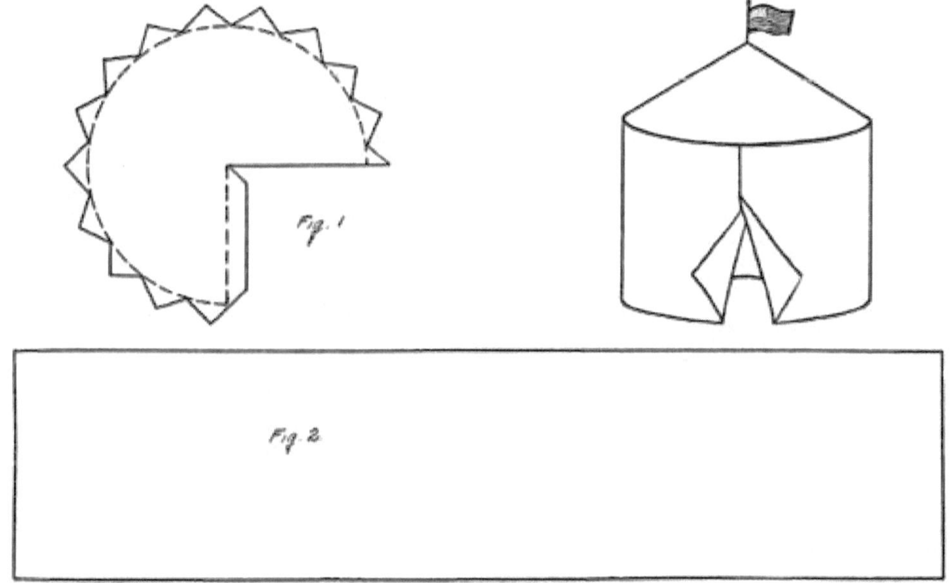

Pattern for Circus Tent.

The animals, next.

There are patterns for them, too, which you will see in the picture and which are so simple as to be very easily enlarged. The animals can be made of the same kind of paper which you used for the tent, and then painted, the elephant gray, the camel a soft brown and the deer a dull reddish color, or you can cut them out of wood. This is perhaps the better way. Use thin pieces of very soft, white wood. An excellent wood is holly or soft pine, in the thin sheets which are used for jig saw work, and for making picture puzzles. Draw the pattern of the animal which you wish to make first very carefully on your piece of wood. Give your best jack-knife two or three turns on a grindstone so that it will be nice and sharp, and then go to work cutting the animal, not your fingers. Make as many animals as you can, and glue their feet to tiny blocks of kindling wood so that they will stand. Touch them up a little with paint, too, to make them look wilder.

If you want cages for your animals use empty spool boxes, covers and all. Cut bars in the cover of each box with your jack-knife, stand the animal inside and put the cover back on. The box rests on cardboard wheels which are glued to the long, narrow side of the box.

A clever boy will be able to invent the acts for the circus. One can rig up trapezes and flying swings and tight rope appliances very easily by using strings and spools. One can paint flags of all nations or cut them from colored tissue paper to float from the roof of the tent, and this little home-made circus will be so attractive that all the other boys will want to make similar ones just as soon as they see it.

BEAD WORK FOR BOYS

THERE is not a boy but has gazed at the alluring Indian suits in the toy shop windows, wishing that he were able to buy one. It is so much easier to give a proper war whoop, and scare a few of the fellows, and execute a wild war dance, or even sit by a camp fire in the woods telling stories, if only he is dressed like a real, live Indian.

Why not make one's own Indian suit?

It is perfectly possible for a boy to make himself a fine Indian shirt, fringed, and decorated with beads; a pair of beaded moccasins and a bead belt in which may be thrust a scalping knife, a bow and arrow and a few other implements of war. He may hang all his scalps to the belt, too.

The only materials needed for the suit will be three or four large chamois skins—or two yards of brown denim if the chamois seems too expensive for the young Indian's pocketbook—some red and blue porcelain beads which may be bought in strings at any dry goods store for a few cents a string, a spool of heavy cotton thread, and a little patience. With a coarse needle, and a pair of scissors the boy will be ready for work. Making an Indian suit will fill a great many rainy afternoons full of fun.

The bead belt is the best part of the suit to begin with because a boy can experiment with designs as he weaves the beads together, and he will be able to form an idea of the pattern he wishes to use when he embroiders the shirt and the moccasins. One will need a bead loom on which to make the belt. These looms may be bought at a toy shop, but that is not really necessary. An old box will do quite as well for a loom. The belt in the picture was started on the cover of an old shoe box, and a cigar box with the cover and the bottom removed makes a fine bead loom. In making a loom from a wooden box, very small screw eyes may be put in the ends of the loom, about one quarter of an inch apart to hold the threads. In the card board cover shown in the picture, the warp threads—those are the lengthwise threads in the weaving—are held in place by pins to which they were knotted at the ends of the loom.

Fourteen threads are strung on the loom for a section of the belt, as tightly as the card board will allow of their being stretched. A needle is then threaded with the coarse cotton thread, and the end is tied to the warp thread at the top of the loom at the left. The needle is then brought out to the right below the warp strands, thirteen red beads—one less bead than the number of the warp strands, remember—are strung on the thread, and the beads are pressed up between the warp strands so that one bead comes between every two threads. The needle is then run back from right to left through the beads *above* the warp threads. This makes one row of beads securely woven to the warp. For the second row of beads, six red beads, one blue one and six more red ones are strung, the blue bead forming the beginning of a simple design. The third row has three blue beads in the center, the fourth has five, the fifth three, and the sixth one, completing the design. A row of red beads is then woven in, after which the unit of design was repeated.

Many different designs will suggest themselves to the boy bead weaver. A checker board pattern of squares may be used, there may be a plain border at the edges of the belt, or a Greek fret may be introduced with charming effect.

When the section of the belt shown in the picture is finished, it may be removed from the loom, the ends of thread being tied securely about the last row of beads. A second section is strung on the loom, blue beads being strung first with a design of red in the center. Four sections, two red and two blue, may be sewed together to complete the gay little Indian belt.

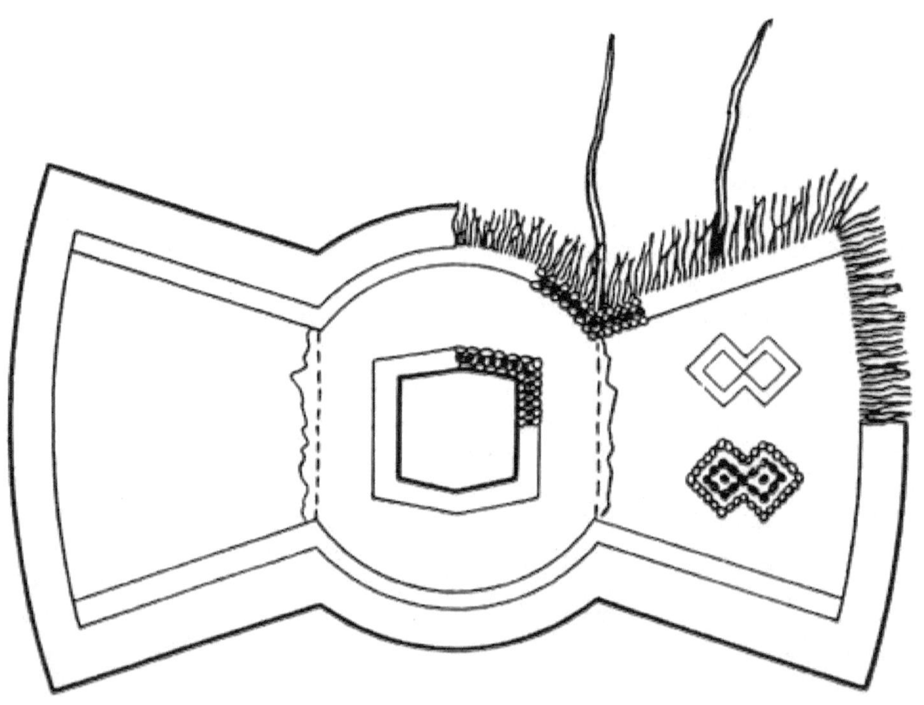

Indian Shirt Pattern.

Now for the Indian's shirt. The pattern which is shown in the picture should be enlarged according to the scale, one and one half inches to a foot. If chamois skin is used for the shirt, probably one large and two smaller skins will need to be joined to give enough material, but if the shirt is made of brown denim, the pattern may be laid on a length of the cloth, without piecing, and the shirt is then cut. It will not be necessary to sew any seams in the shirt. It is folded over at the neck opening, and tied on the small boy with narrow strips of leather indicated in the picture. One strip of leather is tied under the arms, and the other about the hips. The bead embroidery finishes the neck and sides of the shirt. To do this embroidery, a needle is threaded with coarse linen thread, and knotted at the end. Starting at the right of the neck, and close to the edge, the needle is brought through to the outside of the shirt. Three beads are then strung. They are held down close to the shirt and the needle is thrust through the cloth to the inside again. The needle is then brought through, close to the first stitch, three more beads are strung, and the embroidery is continued. Red and blue beads should be alternated to form a design. This stitch described is the simplest one for a boy to use and it is most effective also, being the stitch used by the Indians when they embroidered their own shirts, moccasins, and leggins.

In starting the embroidery for the sides of the shirt, the bead border should be started about two inches from the edge, this margin being fringed carefully with sharp scissors after the beads are all sewed on. A design of beads, which may be varied according to the taste and skill of the boy who makes it, may ornament the front and the back of the shirt.

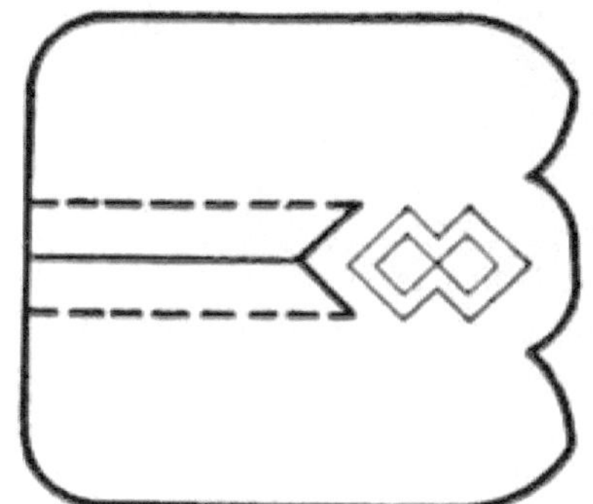 

Moccasin Pattern.Finished Moccasin.

Moccasins sound very difficult to make, but here is a pattern all in one piece, with no troublesome uppers and soles to be fitted together. Chamois skin should be used, if possible, for the moccasins, or the light weight leather which may be bought at a craft shop for art work and can easily be sewed. When the pattern of the moccasin which is shown in the picture has been enlarged according to the scale—three inches to a foot—it is laid on the leather or chamois, and a pair of moccasins is cut out. It will be found easier to embroider the toe before the moccasin is sewed. The sewing which holds the moccasin in shape is done with very coarse thread in an over and over stitch. Narrow strips of leather may be used, also, for the joining, in which case, holes should be punched with a stiletto and awl to admit of the leather being passed through the material. After this joining is completed, the flap indicated in the picture is folded over on the dotted lines, and it is embroidered in the same pattern used to finish the neck and sides of the shirt.

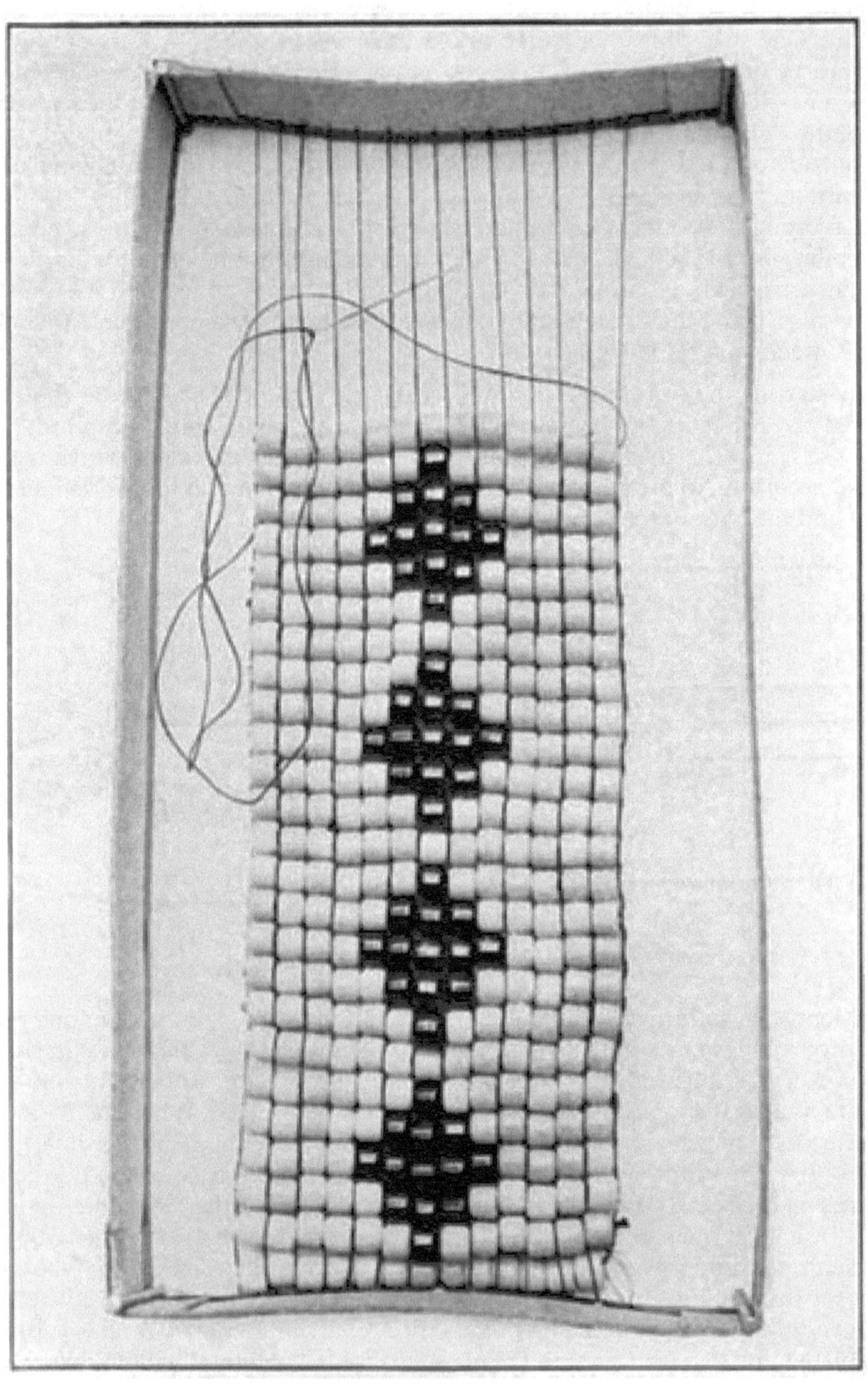

A Bead Loom Made of a Box Cover.

If there is enough of the material that was used for the shirt left, two long, straight pieces may be cut, embroidered on the long edges, fringed, and tied about the Indian's legs for leggins.

A most gorgeous headdress may be made for the Indian from crépe paper feathers. The feathers are made by fringing crépe paper and pasting this fringe to short lengths of flower wire. Gilt paint will make the feathers even more glorious, and when a number of them are finished, red, and blue, and green, and yellow—all the rainbow colors in fact—they may be wired to a headdress made of stiff cambric or heavy cardboard.

What shall we call the boy when he is dressed in his home-made chieftain's suit, which will be more effective, even, than the one he saw in the toy shop? Hiawatha, perhaps, as he dons his war paint and feathers and starts in search of all sorts of interesting Indian adventures.

HOW TO MAKE STICK PICTURES

IT is a new sort of fun that a boy can have with just plain, everyday, ordinary sticks. You can play at being an Indian, too, at the same time for the Indians did it first and called it picture-writing.

Suppose you were an Indian child in paint and feathers, and moccasins. Suppose that you never went to school, and never had seen a piece of paper or a lead pencil. Then suppose that you wanted to write a letter to your little red cousin who lived on the other side of the forest in another tribe, far away from yours.

Of course, you have ever so much to tell your little red cousin. You want him to know that the big chief, your father, has just put up a fine new wigwam of skins for you to live in, a more beautiful wigwam than any other in the village. You want the cousins to know, too, that the sap has begun to run in the maple tree and soon your mother, Laughing Water, will get out the big kettle and build a fire of pine branches and boil the fresh, sweet sap into maple sirup. Then there is a still more wonderful thing to tell your little red cousin. In the full of the last moon, a strange water creature was seen in the river in front of your wigwam. It was white, and large, and it had huge white wings that the wind filled. It was a pale face ship—much larger, and very different from an Indian's canoe.

Now, how are you going to tell all these exciting things to the far-away little red cousin when you have no pencil and no paper for a letter, and there is no post-man and no railway train to carry a letter to the other tribe? Why, it is going to be the easiest thing in the world to do. Make some stick pictures that will tell all the stories that you would like to write if you only knew how.

In the forest there is a fine old hunting ground. You know just the spot where all the tribes gather and build their great camp fires, and cook the game, and dance in the evening when the hunt is done. Before another moon your cousin's tribe will be there. And you are going now, to the hunting ground, to make some stick pictures for that little Indian boy to find. Then he will understand that you have been there and you were thinking of him.

Jump into your canoe and paddle down the river. Tie the canoe fast to the bank, then jump out and plunge into the forest. You know the way to go, for the moss grows on the north side of the trees. There, you have come to a cleared spot in the deep, deep woods. There isn't any sound save the chattering of the chipmunks. They won't disturb your picture writing. Now you may go to work.

You break many of the straight, stout twigs from the pine tree. Some of the twigs must be long, and others you will break off short to fit together where there are corners in the pictures. There is a smooth bed of moss under the pine tree. That will be a splendid place for your picture writing. First, you will make a picture of the new wigwam. Just two long sticks, crossed at the top will make the outline, and you put two short sticks together to show the door. Now, for the maple tree. You will lay a long stick down on the moss to show the outline of the tree. Some shorter sticks, laid close to the sides of the longer stick make the branches. The pale face ship may be more difficult to make, but you will be able to outline the picture with your sticks. There are the sloping sides of the ship and there are the sails.

The picture letter is done. When the little cousin finds it there in the woods he will know all about the new wigwam, and the maple sirup, and the strange ship. You travel home again if you are a little Indian boy, and you don't mind in the least not having a pencil, or a postman.

How may a little pale face child play at picture writing?

If it is vacation time, you can gather sticks in the woods just as the little Indian boy did. Be sure that they are long, straight ones, though. You may sit in the grass and lay your stick pictures on the lawn, or you may make them on the floor of the piazza.

If you want to make stick pictures in the house on a stormy day, ask mother to let you use her sewing table to put them on, or you can lay them on the kitchen floor, or the nursery hearth rug. For the indoor stick pictures, you can use burnt matches, or toothpicks, or clothes pins—anything long and straight will do. You can buy colored sticks at a kindergarten shop, and those will be the best of all for stick pictures. And if you have a game of jackstraws, the straws may be used for the pictures.

The Indians had no picture books, but you have. You can play a game with the stick pictures. You can make pictures to illustrate one of your favorite stories, and then ask the boy or girl who is playing with you to try and guess what the story is that fits the picture.

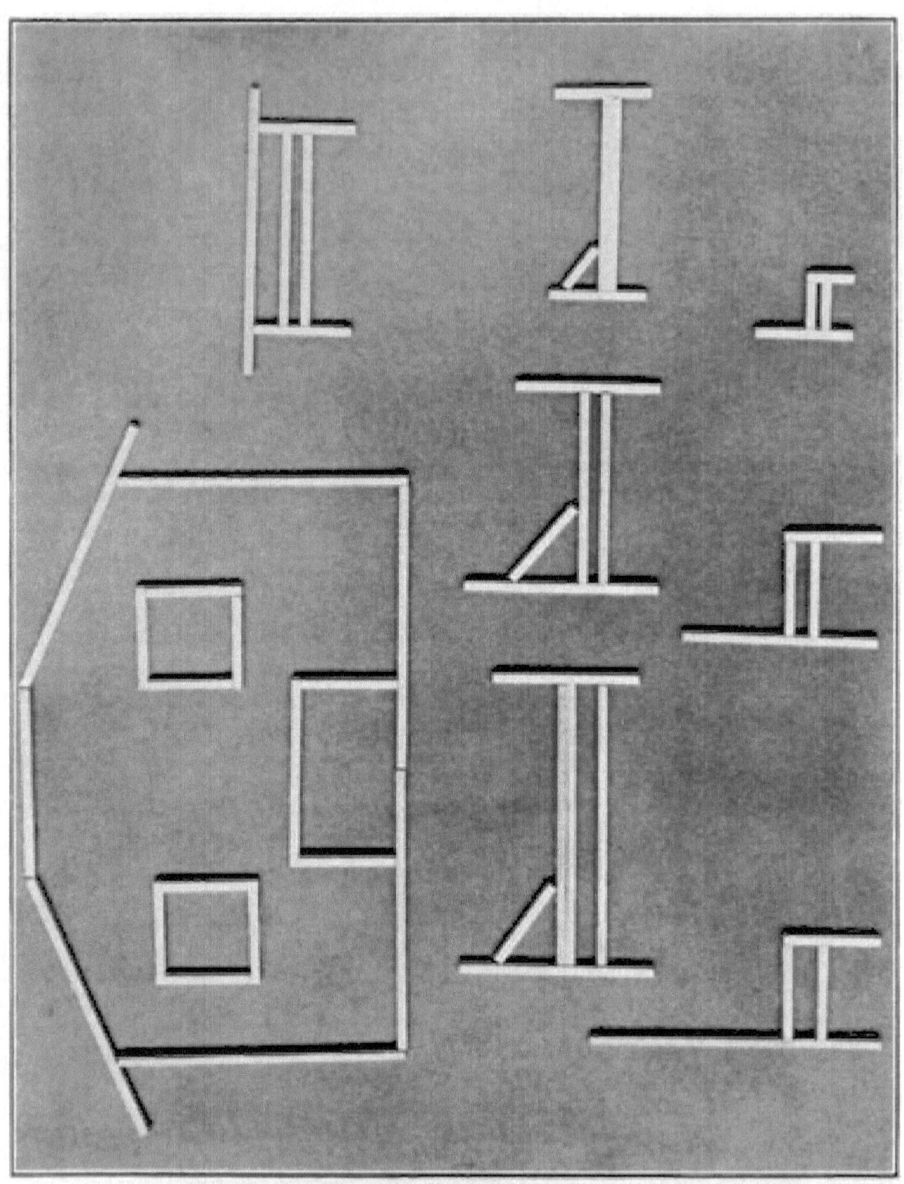

Stick Illustration of the Story of The Three Bears.

A splendid story to illustrate with stick pictures is The Three Bears.

Here is their house.

Here is the table that held the three bowls of porridge.

Here are their three chairs.

And here are their three beds.

A TOY INDIAN VILLAGE

JUST fancy an encampment of real, live Indians in the house in a little Indian village that you made all yourself! It will be the best sort of fun to make the camp, and when it is done it will be a fine, new plaything for all winter long, as the toy Indians have sham fights, and May dances and tell each other stories around their tiny camp fires. And this is the way to make the fascinating toy.

A long, shallow tin with very narrow sides is the foundation for the Indian village. The tinsmith has large sheets of bright new tin, and he will make you one of these shallow tin trays for just a few cents. The florist will give you a basket of soft, black earth—enough to fill the tray—and you can mold and pat it into tiny hills and queer little valleys, and long foot paths, no wider than your little finger for the toy Indians to trail up and down.

You must take a long walk now as far as the woods to find some sprays of white pine, hemlock, and spruce for the Indians' trees. Gather some little straight twigs, too, for wigwam foundations, and if the ground is still bare, pick up some of the prettiest pebbles you can find for make-believe rocks in the Indian encampment. With your jack-knife strip from the birch tree just a very little bark to make an Indian canoe—not much, for it takes a birch a long, long time to grow more bark. Then you may go home again, but on the way, buy a penny's worth of grass seed at the florist's. What are you to do with all these things?

Just listen, and you will find out.

Scatter the grass seed very softly over the earth in your tray and sprinkle it with the rubber bulb sprayer that mother uses for her house ferns. You would not believe it perhaps, but in a week or ten days your little Indian camp ground will be covered with a carpet of soft, green grass really growing in the earth. After you have planted the grass seed, stick the little evergreen trees in the earth and lay your pebbles about as if they really belonged there on the ground. In one corner of the tray, if mother is willing, you may sink a shallow, round cake tin filled with water to make a miniature lake, and about the lake you can put a border of stones covered with the moss that comes in a box of Noah's Ark animals. The tray of earth is quite transformed now into a tiny forest.

Under the trees the Indian wigwams are scattered. Making these tepees is ever so much fun and will fill a long winter evening after your lessons are learned and you have the library table free to work on. Fig. 1 shows you how to cut out an Indian wigwam, and heavy dark brown paper or brown canvas is a strong material to use. When the wigwam is cut, it may be decorated with paints in any design you wish. A border of small squares is an attractive decoration, or some grotesque heads and bows and arrows may be painted on. Gold or red paper stars and crescents and suns may be cut and glued to the outside of the wigwam, forming a very gay scheme of trimming it, or very tiny autumn leaves may be waxed and glued on. When a number of these little wigwams have been cut, decorated, and glued together, as shown in Fig. 2, place them in your play forest, using two or three twigs crossed for supports, the ends extending through the hole in the top of the wigwam.

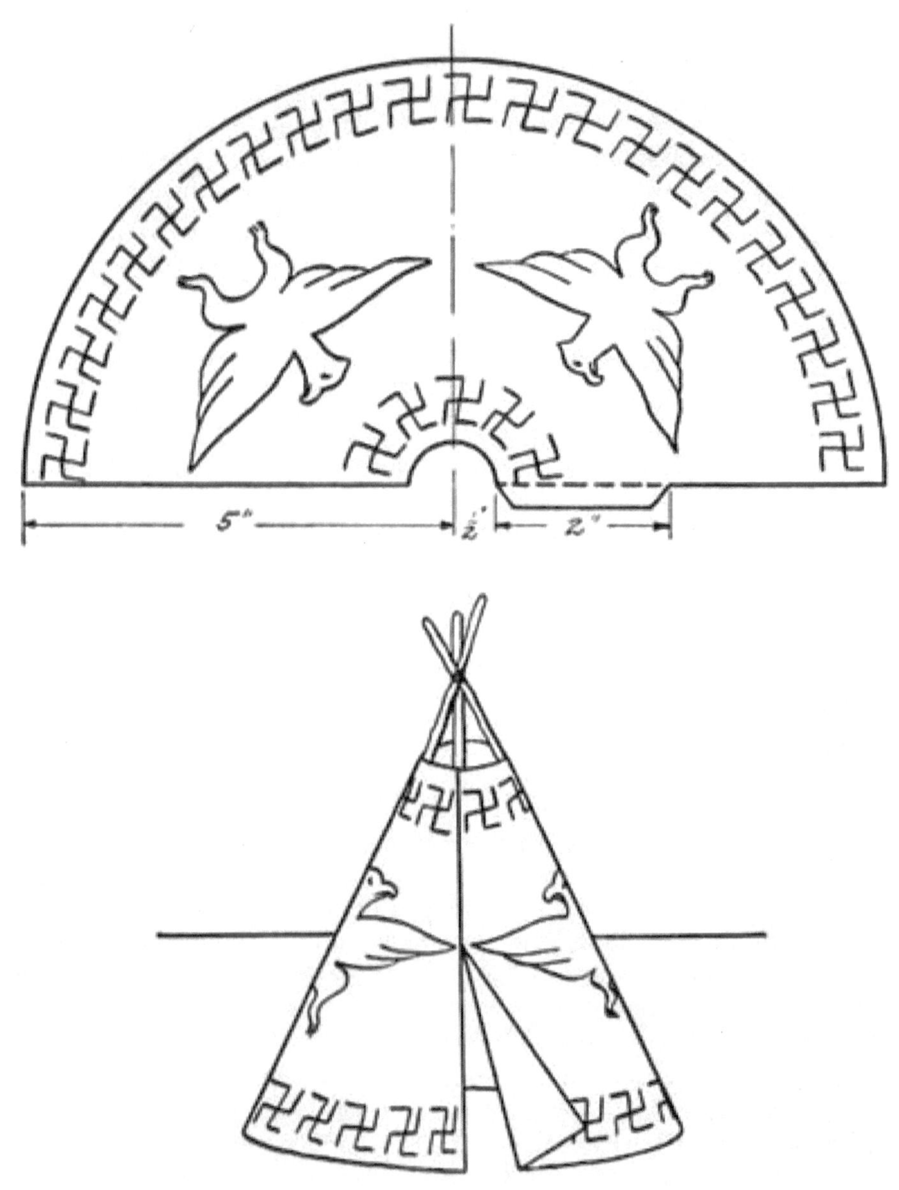

Pattern for Toy Wigwam.

Now you can make the Indians. English walnuts form the heads. These are just the right size, brown enough for the complexion of any Indian, and nicely wrinkled, too. With a sharp jack-knife smooth down a few of the walnut's wrinkles, and carve the Indian's features, trying to give him high cheek bones. Color his cheeks with vermilion and paint his face, too, in as many different colors as you like. A roll of stiff paper or cloth glued to the nut head makes the Indian's body, about which is wrapped a blanket of fringed crépe paper, red flannel, or any sort of gay stuff that mother will give you. This walnut Indian wears a marvelous feather headdress. The feathers come from the chicken yard or the oldest feather duster—whichever source is available—and they are glued to a strip of brown paper which, in turn is glued to the little Indian's head.

There should be a whole tribe of Indians, as many as you can make before bed-time, and when it comes morning run up to the play room and stand the Indian braves at the doors of their wigwams or in the little path between the trees where they can see their real green grass coming up, and enjoy the friendly shelter of their fine little camping ground.

These nut Indians will need bows and arrows when they have sham battles. Tiny twigs may be bent bow shape with rubber bands for bow strings and burned out matches may be sharpened to a point for arrows. Toothpicks make arrows, too. A bow and a bundle of arrows may be laid at the door of each little Indian's wigwam. The canoe that floats on the tin pan lake is made of a strip of folded birch bark shaped at the ends like a real canoe and stitched with brown linen thread. It will really float if it is carefully made.

For a camp fire, pile up some broken twigs in a cleared spot in your Indian encampment and put in some scraps of twisted, red tissue paper which will look like flames. One of the kettles from the dolls' kitchen may hang on a forked stick over this make-believe fire to cook the dinner for the walnut Indian tribe.

This play Indian village will last all winter, a comfortable camping ground for the tribe, and a delightful plaything for the clever boy who made it.

There may be some walnut squaws added perhaps, and some peanut papooses wrapped in blankets cut from a scrap of old chamois and hung contentedly by thread to the sheltering trees. The grass will grow so high that it may have to be mowed with the nursery scissors, and when the trees fade, more can be gathered and put in the places of the old ones.

CORN TOYS AND HOW TO MAKE THEM

CORN cobs really look as if they would like to play. There is a whole binful out in the barn, and the chickens do not want them and neither does the farmer. He will make a big bonfire out in the wood lot some day and burn up all the corn cobs if the children do not take possession of them first, and help them to play by making them into toys.

What fine, long, straight little logs they are for a log cabin, or they might be made into Indian or toy rafts, or a rail fence, or almost anything else a child chooses.

First you can make a little rail fence that stretches across one corner of the barn floor. To do this, lay down six corn cobs in zigzag fashion on the floor with the ends not quite as far apart as the cobs are long. Then across every two cob ends lay another cob and finish the fence in this way, making it very snug.

Behind the fence lives Apple Johnny. He owns the farm whose boundary lines the fence marks out on the floor. Apple Johnny has a little hard apple for his head joined by a toothpick to a fat apple that forms his body. His legs and arms are twigs and his face is cut with a jack-knife in the smaller apple. Apple Johnny has a herd of wild potato horses on his farm. Each potato has four twig legs, and a flowing mane, made of a fringed corn husk pinned to the long end of the potato, and a straw tail pinned to the other end.

As you put the last corn cob in the fence, you heard the rain just pouring and pouring on the barn eaves. Suppose the roof of the barn should cave in and the whole inside be flooded! What would poor little Apple Johnny do, and how would he ever make his escape? Apple Johnny must have a raft. Select six more corn cobs from the binful, all of them just the same length, and lay them down on the barn floor, side by side. In one of the corners of the barn is an old last summer's berry basket. Strip off two bits of the binding rim as long as the row of cobs is wide. Nail one to each end of the row of corn cobs, putting a nail in each cob, which holds the small raft firmly in place. Then turn the raft right side up and to one end nail a long, straight twig for a mast, to which you can glue a white paper sail. It is a fine little raft when it is completed, and strong enough to carry Apple Johnny and a potato horse or two safely through any possible flood.

But Apple Johnny has no house. Well, a house is easily planned when one has a whole bin of corn cobs to draw upon for building materials.

Gather an armful of cobs and make a corn-cob house. Lay two corn cobs opposite each other, and two more across the ends, log cabin fashion, driving nails through to hold them together. Next, put two more corn cobs over the first two and two more over the second, until the house is twice as high as Apple Johnny is tall. For a roof, nail two sides of the berry basket to the log cabin, and then with a rip saw cut out a front door high enough to let Apple Johnny step through. There will be rather wide chinks in the house, but you can play that these are windows through which Apple Johnny can watch for the corn-cob Indians and shoot at them with a twig musket when he sees them coming.

You can make a whole tribe of these corn-cob Indians, and it will be the most fun of all, even jollier than making a corn-cob fence, and a raft, and a house. First, wind corn husks around a cob to make the Indian's clothes, but leave one end, the larger end of the cob, uncovered because that is going to be the Indian's head. Then on this end, mark a face with a bit of charcoal; eyes, nose, and mouth; and paint the cheeks red with a crushed cranberry, rubbing the juice on the corn cob. The hens' nests in the barn are full of ever so many pretty feathers, so you can collect as many of these as you wish and glue them to the corn-cob Indian's head for his headdress. Last of all, ask mother if she is willing to give you a few pieces of the left over plain cloth from sister's school dress for the corn-cob Indian's blanket. Of course mother is willing. Almost every mother is willing to give a boy things when he is trying to amuse himself all alone. She may even cut a square of gay plaid from the piece of cloth itself and turn out all the pieces from her sewing bag, where there are other scraps just right for Indians' blankets; red flannel, and gray serge like your last winter suit, and brown merino, and yellow silk.

The Indian looks very splendid indeed in his feather headdress and a red plaid blanket. All he needs then is a bow and quiver of arrows. The bow you can make by bending a length of willow and tying a piece of cord across. The arrows are shorter, pointed twigs with a very small hen's feather tied to the end of each.

This Indian you can name Chief Big Cob.

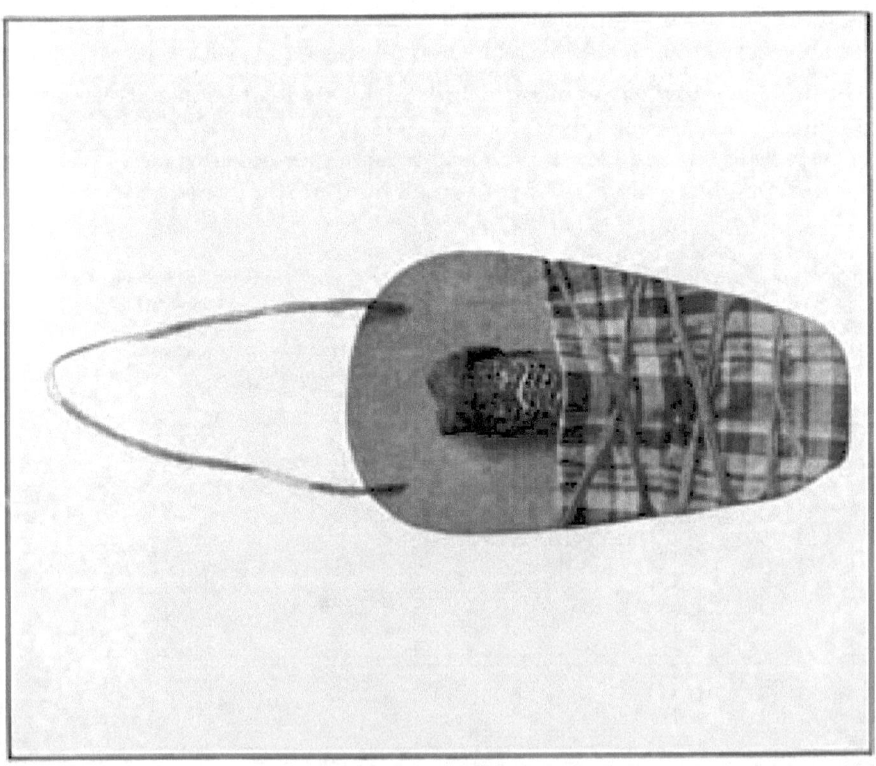

Corn Cob Pappoose Corn Cob Indian.

HOW TO MAKE A MARBLE BAG

NOBODY knows why the first of March brings marbles, but it certainly does. Some games really belong to the season in which they come as coasting and snowfights, but other games are played at certain times of the year for no reason except that they always have been and always will be. If some one should ask a boy—any boy, why it wouldn't be better to play football in the summer and baseball at Thanksgiving time, he couldn't tell you, but his sense of the fitness of things would be outraged.

And so, when the snow goes away, and the frost comes out of the ground, and the sap begins to run in the trees, and a boy's toes wiggle and wiggle and long to kick out of his shoes and dig themselves into the soft mud, it is quite the proper thing for him to hunt up all his last year's marbles, and ask his sister—or somebody else's sister—to make him a bag to hold them, so that he will be ready for the season's marble campaign.

The simplest marble bag to make is one which is made in just the same way as a tobacco pouch. Take an oblong piece of heavy tan canvas, measuring twelve inches long by five inches wide. Tan does not show the dirt readily, and the heavier the material is the better, for the bag is not going to be gently handled. Double this piece of canvas in the center, so that it forms a bag six inches deep by five wide. Sew up the two side seams with a coarse needle and very heavy linen thread, and make the seams very strong. The sewing should be about a quarter of an inch back from the edges. Then "scrape" the seams open, which simply means to run your thumb nail along the seams right where the joining is, so that one raw edge shall be folded toward each side. Next make a hem at the top by folding the material over once, and then again. This hem should be about a quarter of an inch wide, and in sewing it down leave a space unsewed on one side where it crosses the seam, so that the draw string can be run in. Turn your bag so that it will be right side out, and the seaming all on the inside. A piece of heavy, wrapping-paper twine twelve inches long will make a fine draw string, by running it through the hem with a bodkin and tying the two ends together.

Another marble bag that will prove very satisfactory, and will be so unusual that the boy who owns it can gloat over the other fellows, is made of very heavy chamois, or buckskin. A paper pattern is made first, like Fig. 1. It measures two and a half inches across the top, four and a half inches from side to side at a point three and three-quarters inches below the top, and its height is six and a half inches. After these points have been determined a boy can mark in the vase shaped outline freehand. When the pattern is made and cut out, lay it on the buckskin, holding it carefully, so that it will not slip, and cut four pieces just alike. Then take a large darning needle or a "rug" needle and thread it with a strand of raffia. If red, or blue, or green raffia are used instead of the ordinary natural color, it will make the sewing very decorative. Take two of the pieces of buckskin, and, beginning at the bottom, sew them together with the stitch that is used for making baseballs. This is done by taking a stitch up from underneath, then crossing over, and taking a stitch up from the under side of the other piece, then back to the first piece and so on, drawing the raffia snug each time. Instead of making a knot at the beginning, leave the raffia hanging loose for about an inch or more, and when the top of the seam is reached, fasten the raffia tight before cutting off. Next join the third piece to the second in the same way, the fourth to the third, and then the fourth to the first, so that all four together form a bag. Take the four ends of raffia at the bottom and knot them snugly together, two by two. They may be trimmed off short, or left hanging loose to form a tassel for decoration. Now take a narrow piece of soft wood and slip it inside the mouth of the bag, so that you can cut slits for the draw string. They are cut with a sharp penknife and should come just at the narrowest part, or neck of the bag. If the upper ends of the cuts are three-quarters of an inch from the top of the bag, and the cuts themselves a half inch long, they will be about right. There are four cuts in each section making sixteen cuts in all. Next take three pieces of raffia twenty-four inches long. Knot the three together at one end, and then braid them tightly into a cord. When the other end is reached knot it as you did the first. String this cord through the slits in the neck of the bag just as though you were weaving—under one, over one, under one, over one—and then when it is all strung, tie the two ends together in a square knot.

It makes an exceedingly unique bag, and will hold all the marbles a boy can win, and besides winning marbles he will win the envy of every other boy who sees his fine, new marble bag.

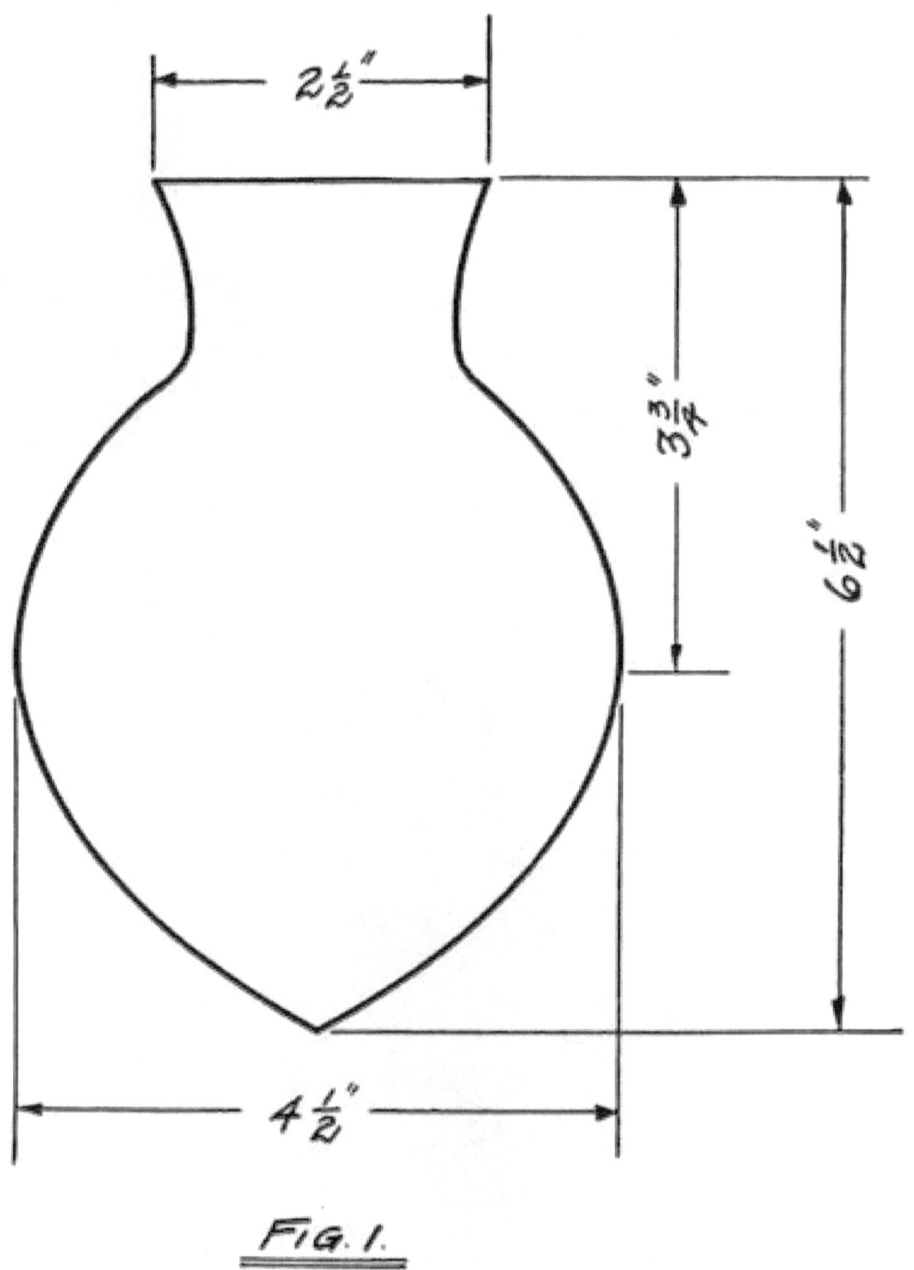

Pattern of a Marble Bag.

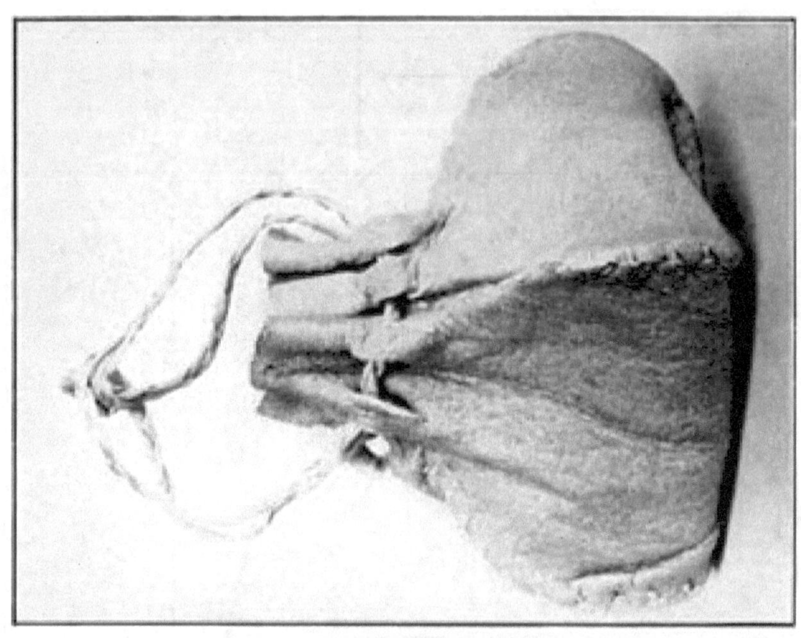

Whittled School Box Chamois Marble Bag.

HOW TO MAKE YOUR OWN SCHOOL BOX

EVERY boy needs a pencil box. Plain little oblong boxes most of them, with a flat hinged cover, and a little lock that you keep carefully fastened with the key. That is, a boy locks his pencil box when he is able to find the key, but whether it was in his pocket, or fastened to his watch chain, the school-box key always does manage to get away, somewhere—to make its escape.

One day, however, the boy sees displayed in the window of a stationery shop, a new sort of pencil box, a most fascinating kind. The cover of the box is made of narrow strips of wood fastened side by side like the strips in the top of a roll-top desk, and when the shopman opens the pencil box to show the boy the inside, the cover just *slides* right back out of sight, while the boy looks on in open-eyed astonishment. The shopman's supply of these magic boxes is limited, though, and there is a wild scramble for their possession among the boys who can produce ten cents—for that is the exorbitant price charged by the shopman. The boy wants one of those magic boxes. His fingers just tingle and burn to hold one and try to make the cover slide in its charming way, but he has only five cents, he can't buy one.

The boy will be able to make his own pencil box, though, and this is the way he must go about it in order to construct one of those fascinating, roll-top ones, just like the one in the shop window.

In the first place, a boy must know how to whittle. All that he needs in the way of material is a jack-knife, some pieces of wood three-sixteenths of an inch thick, some more pieces an eighth thick, a strip of white cloth, and some little three-eighth inch nails.

The first piece to make (Fig. 1) is the side of the box. It is just a plain oblong of the three-sixteenth inch wood, measuring nine inches long by two and a quarter inches wide. All the pieces are made three-sixteenths thick except the strips for the cover. Two of these sides are necessary of course.

Next come two strips nine inches long and a quarter of an inch wide which are fastened, notched side up on the inside of each side, "flush"—even—that is, with the top, with four little nails driven from the outside. The piece which is cut from the end of each of these, as shown in the drawing, is to make a joint which is later to be fitted with Fig. 10.

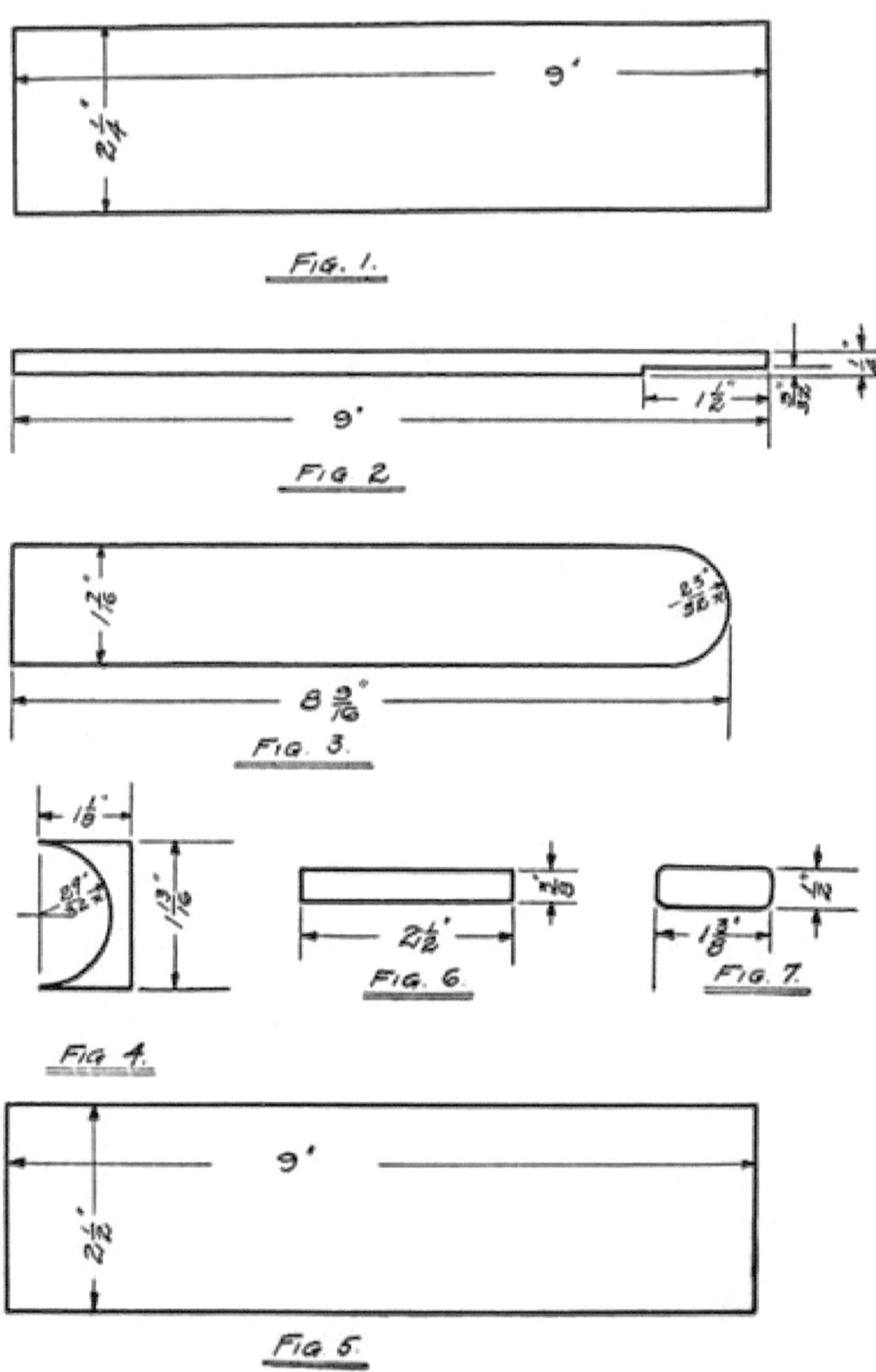

Diagrams of a School Box.

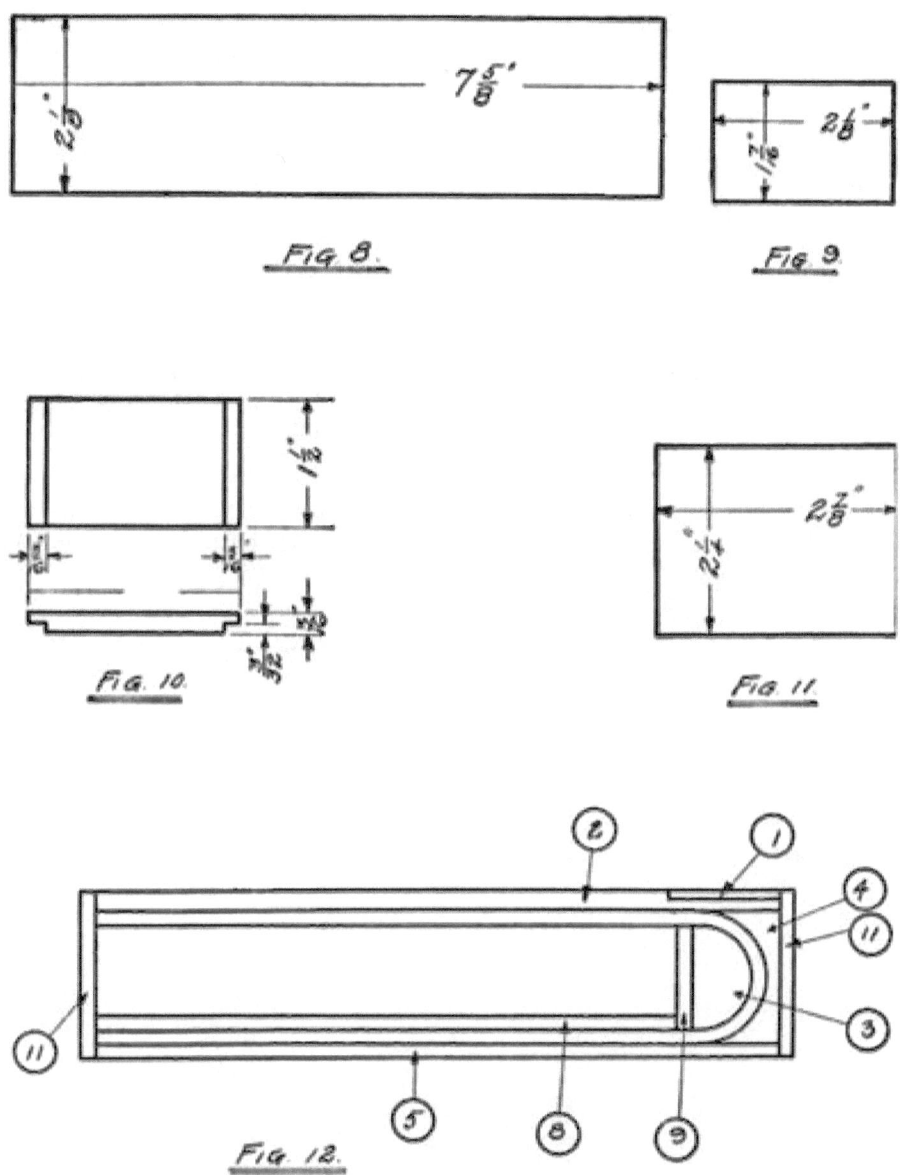

Diagrams of a School Box.

Fig. 3 is eight and nine-sixteenths inches long and one and seven-sixteenths wide and one end is rounded into a half circle. Figs. 3 and 4 are nailed in position on the inside of the side pieces, and together they form the track around which the cover runs. Two of each are required. Fig. 5 is the bottom piece, and is simply an oblong nine inches long by two and a half wide. It is placed in position with the side pieces upright on either side of it and nailed from the outside.

It is best to make the cover next, so that you can test it and see that it works smoothly before any more of the box is put together. It is made of little strips (Fig. 6) three-eighths of an inch wide and two and a half inches long, "sliding fit," which means that they are to be a little less than two and a half, so that they will slide in a space two and a half inches wide. A sharp rub on the ends with sandpaper will make this slight difference. There are twenty-two of these strips, and they are glued side by side on a strip of white muslin cloth. If you use a piece with a selvage on one side, you will be more sure of making the cover perfectly straight.

Fig. 7 is the handle and is to be nailed flat to the second strip—the one next to the end strip.

Fig. 8 and Fig. 9 are a false bottom and false end, which form the receptacle for the pencils, and hide the mechanism of the cover. They are nailed in position as shown in Fig. 12. The nails to fasten these in place must be a little longer than the others, because they have to be nailed from the outside and must go through two thicknesses of wood and project into a third.

The next piece to make is Fig. 10—an oblong measuring one and a half inches by two and a half, and cut to make a joint with Fig. 2. This is placed across the top and nailed down, covering the rounding end of the "track."

Now the cover may be slipped into position and the end pieces (Fig. 11), oblongs two and a quarter inches by two and seven-eighths, nailed on, and the box is done.

It is a convenient size, the receptacle for pencils is ample, and to one who does not know, the disappearance of that cover when it opens is a mystery that borders on black art.

A HOME-MADE CHRISTMAS TREE STAND

NOBODY will deny that a Christmas tree has plenty of backbone, but somehow it doesn't seem to have intelligence enough to use it. Or else it resents the taking away of its roots and the substitution of a shop-made standard that it considers inadequate. As a matter of fact the standards that you can buy in the shops *are* inadequate for a tree of any size. And so, if the boy of the family is handy with tools, it is up to him to make one.

A very good standard for a Christmas tree—strong, durable, and ornamental as well—may be made from a strip of one-by-two-inch "dressed" lumber 12 ft. long (which costs about a cent and a half a foot), and some pieces of an old dry goods box.

First, saw off from your one-by-two-inch strip four pieces twelve inches long and four pieces eleven inches. These are to make Figs. 1, 2, and 4. Make four pieces like Fig. 1 and two pieces like Fig. 2; the notch at the end is cut with a saw across the grain, and then split out with a chisel.

When these are done, join two of the twelve-inch pieces and two of the eleven inch to form a square frame. The joint is shown in Fig. 3, and it should be glued or nailed, or both, which is safer.

Next make the other two eleven-inch pieces like Fig. 4. These are just like Fig. 2 except that a groove four inches wide and one inch deep is cut in the middle of each. Then they are joined with the other twelve-inch pieces to form a frame similar to the first. The first frame is to go at the bottom of the standard, and the second frame, placed with the grooves *up*, is for the top.

Now cut from the remainder of the strip two more pieces twelve inches long. With a compass set at an inch-and-a-half radius, and the center in the exact middle of one edge, draw a half circle on each, and chip it out with a chisel like Fig. 5. The use of these will be described later.

The remainder of the strip will make four pieces eighteen inches long, with a bit left over. These are to stand on their two-inch faces, and the upper edges of each end should be rounded off with a "block" plane. Then two grooves are cut in each piece, two of the pieces having the grooves on the upper side and two on the under side, like Figs. 6 and 7.

Now cut from your packing box sixteen strips or pickets one and three-quarters inches wide and fourteen inches long, like Fig. 8. These may be "ripped out" with a saw and smoothed up with a plane and sandpaper.

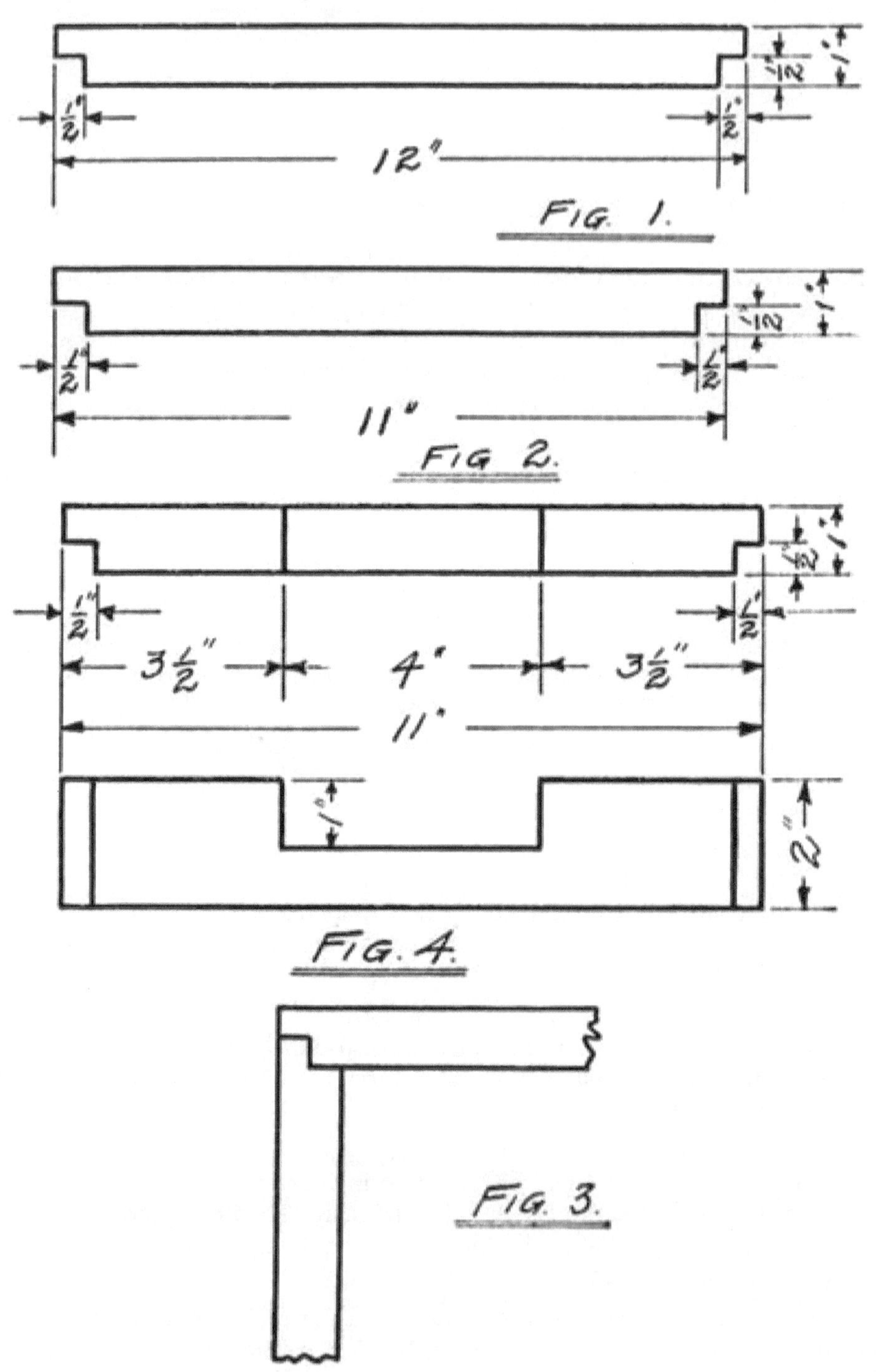

Diagrams of a Christmas Tree Stand.

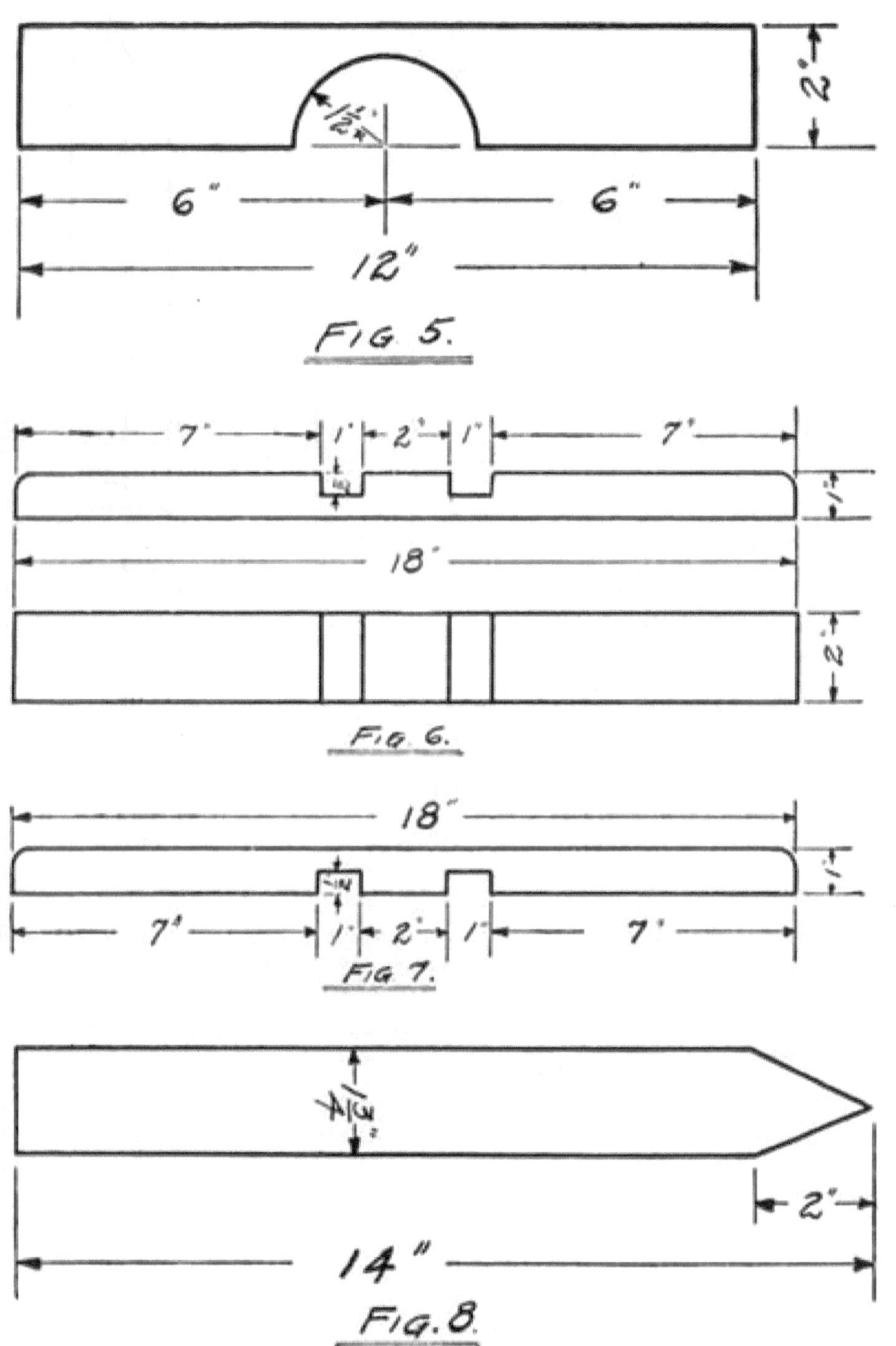

Diagrams of a Christmas Tree Stand.

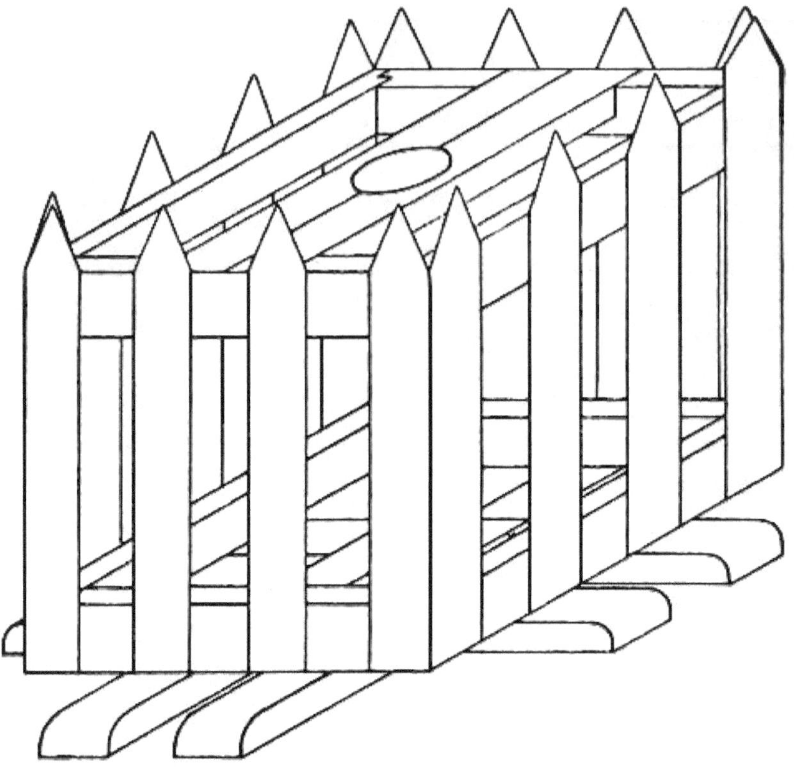

Christmas Tree Stand.

To "assemble" the standard join first the two Fig. 6 strips and two Fig. 7. This leaves a hole two inches square in the center and two strips projecting from each of the four sides. Place the first square frame that you made on this, so that its sides will be equally distant from the center, and nail in position. Next nail the pickets in position so that the lower end of the pickets will be "flush" with the lower side of the frame. Next, hold the upper frame, with the grooves up, in position, eight inches above the lower frame and nail the pickets to that. Fig. 9 shows the complete assembly.

Now give the frame, and the two pieces like Fig. 5 a coat of dark green paint, and the standard is ready for use. Slip the tree into the square hole in the base. If the trunk is a bit too large, whittle it to fit. Then place the two pieces like Fig. 5 around the trunk at the top of the frame for a clamp, and slip them into the grooves in the upper frame, and you will find your tree quite ready to stand up and behave.

HOW TO WRAP CHRISTMAS PARCELS

HOW many boys and big folks, too, have at some time received a Christmas gift which was broken, or crushed, or spoiled in some way through the careless packing of the sender. Even at ordinary times the mail service and Express Companies are hard enough upon packages given to their care. The term "baggage-smasher" ought not to be restricted to the employees of the railways alone, and when at Christmas time the mails and express lines are congested with packages of all descriptions, and the men are tired and overworked trying to deliver gifts that have been sent at the last minute—then it is doubly needful to insure the safety of your Christmas presents by careful packing.

Of course the wrapping of a gift cannot change its value, but you should bear in mind that your gift will *seem* doubly attractive to the one who receives it, if inside of the serviceable outside wrapping, there is another dainty one, and the expense is so trifling that it need hardly be considered. A dozen sheets of tissue paper cost only a dime. Pure white or warm "Christmassy" red are the most desirable kinds. Another dime will purchase a box of Christmas seals—small ones with pictures of holly and mistletoe, or large ones with Santa Claus heads or Christmas bells on them. If you prefer tying, to sealing, the ten cents will buy a dozen yards of "tying" ribbon, which is crimson "baby" ribbon in a cheaper grade than is ordinarily sold. Gilt cord is also very attractive for tying up gifts, and a tiny spray of holly tucked under the cord or ribbon gives a final dainty Christmas touch.

Perhaps, though, you live so far away from a town that you are not able to buy these Christmas seals, and the tying ribbon. Almost, if not quite as pretty to fasten the inside tissue paper wrapping of a gift will be some very tiny, red maple leaves gathered in the fall with the thought of Christmas in mind, and pressed with a hot flat iron on which some beeswax has been rubbed. This preserves the bright color of the leaves and keeps them stiff until you need to use them. After carefully folding in the ends of the tissue paper about the gift, the paper is fastened down by gluing on a few of these gay, pressed leaves, and in the folds of the paper a wee spray of pine or a little wreath made of ground pine, or a bunch of partridge berries may be tucked. Another way of making a gift look like the country is to tie it with strands of sweet grass.

When the gifts are wrapped, and you are ready to pack them for shipment, there are a few general rules that must be remembered.

First: That the gifts must be packed as snugly as it is possible to do without harming them.

Second: That nothing—not even excelsior—is quite as effective in stopping the transmission of bumps and jars as crumpled up newspapers.

Third: That the name and address of the person to whom the gift is sent and also the address of the sender must be legibly written in your best school hand on the outer covering where they are not liable to be torn off. You must remember that, while the names and addresses are perfectly familiar to you, they are totally unknown to the men through whose hands the parcels go, and in handling thousands of packages, illegible writing means much delay.

The rule of packing things tightly refers to *everything*—even things which would seem most crushable, for there is far more harm done by packing these loosely so that they slip around with every turn of the package, than by crushing them flat in one position. Take a delicate waist, for instance. If packed loosely, it will come out of its box rumpled and wrinkled in every direction, but if it is folded flat, the sleeves stuffed with crumpled tissue paper, and the spaces around it in the box filled with the same, it will reach its destination quite as fresh as when it started.

It is better to *box* all gifts if possible. Very pretty Christmas boxes of all sizes and shapes may be bought in the shops, or, in place of these, you can use empty candy boxes which most people stow away for just such purposes.

Do not select a box that is too small and leaves too little space for filling in with crushed paper, and try and think, too, of the weight of the gift in selecting your box.

If you are packing odd pieces of china, wrap each piece separately, and see that they are well segregated with the crushed paper. If you are packing a number of pieces of uniform size and shape—such as saucers, plates, etc.—place them in a pile with every *second* one well wrapped. Then wrap the whole pile and pack *edgewise*.

China should be packed in a wooden box, with an addressed baggage tag nailed on, or the address put on the wood itself with India ink.

Flat things, calendars, cards, photographs, and handkerchiefs, gloves, neckties, ribbons, etc. if unboxed, must be protected by pasteboard. For this, the corrugated pasteboard that is used by department stores is much more effective than the ordinary flat sort. It is much less easily bent, and is lighter in weight, which is of course a great advantage, because it makes the cost of mailing less.

This corrugated pasteboard is also very good for wrapping things which are light in weight, but bulky and of awkward shape, for it may be rolled to accommodate almost any object.

Doilies, centerpieces, and other flat embroideries must necessarily be kept uncreased in shipping, but are too large to be sent flat. Lay them first on a sheet of heavy wrapping paper, cut square and slightly larger than the embroidered piece. Then lay over the embroidery a sheet of tissue paper, and carefully roll the whole thing. Then form a tubular covering of the corrugated pasteboard, and wrap with hardware paper outside. In tying up a tube, the cord should go twice around the tube—once near each end—and the cord which goes lengthwise should go through the opening of the tube so that the contents will not slip out.

In tying packages for mailing, use good strong cord, and remember that a package must bear no kind of a seal and contain no kind of writing beyond a simple Christmas greeting if it is to go as "merchandise." Even one of the little paper seals stuck over the string will render the package "first class" and subject to letter postage.

Just one more thing to be remembered at Christmas time. Courtesy is only another name for kindness, and it would be discourteous to send a gift which was not fully prepaid; or to send a gift "across the line," which is dutiable to any great extent. And in courtesy to the men and women who have to handle your gifts on their journeys, send your Christmas presents long enough ahead of time so that these men and women may not be too tired when Christmas comes to feel themselves its blessed peace and cheer.

YOUR OWN WIRELESS RECEIVING STATION

MOST boys are interested in wireless telegraphy, and it is possible for any one of them to make a simple apparatus by which they can "cut in" and receive any wireless message that happens to be passing through their particular zone.

The receiving set will require a number of different parts, but they are easily made—when one knows how.

For actual hearing you will need a telephone receiver of some sort. One may be bought for about seventy-five cents at an electrical supply house, or an old one, provided it is in good condition, may be used.

Next comes a "detector." This consists of a wooden base about six inches long by four wide and an inch thick, on which is mounted a piece of silicon about the size of an egg. An insulated wire passed once around the silicon and then through two holes in the base will hold the silicon in position in the center of the block. Put a brass screw an inch long at each end of the block and "connect up" the silicon in the following way: First take a piece of No. 22 single-covered copper wire, scrape off a few inches of the covering, and wind this bare copper wire several times around a small round stick to form a spring. The bare end of the spring must be filed to a point and rest against one end of the silicon, while the other end of the wire is wound around one of the brass screws. Next, take a piece of ordinary insulated telephone wire, bare one end far enough to wind firmly around the free end of the piece of silicon, and then wind the other end of this wire around the second brass screw. This makes a metallic circuit through the silicon which will "make" or "break" with the touching or removing of the spring.

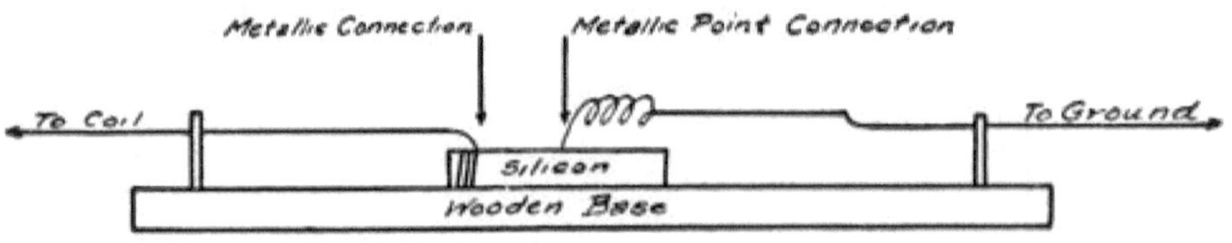

Detector.

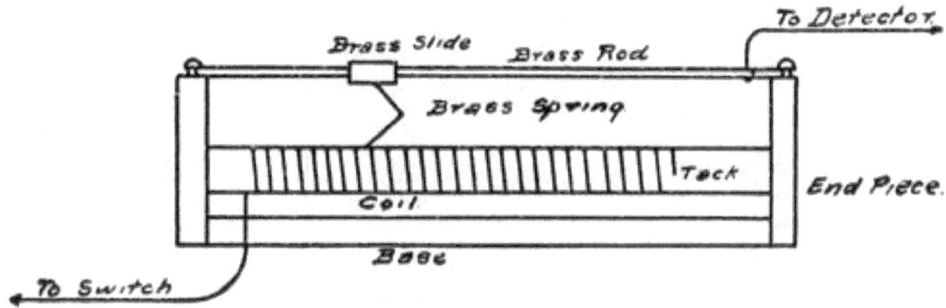

Tuning Coil.

Next you need a "tuning coil." This has a wooden base twelve inches by six and an inch thick. To make the coil itself a stick twelve inches long and one and a half inches in diameter—a piece of an old curtain pole will do—and wind carefully on it a half pound of the No. 22 single-covered copper wire. The end of this wire is fastened to the stick with a small tack, and it should be wound very evenly and closely. The last end is left free for a connection. After it is wound give the wire three coats of shellac, making sure that each coat is dry before another one is put on. When it is thoroughly dry mark two straight lines from end to end, a quarter of an inch apart. With a sharp knife scrape off the insulation so that the wires are bare on the outside, but be careful not to disturb the insulation between the wires. To mount the coil, nail at each end a wooden strip three inches wide, three and a half high and one inch thick. This has also to be nailed to the base, and it should be placed so that the coil will clear the base by a half inch. The strip of bare wire on the coil should be uppermost. Now get a brass rod one quarter of an inch square and thirteen inches long; a thin brass strip one quarter inch wide and two inches long; another strip one inch wide and one and one-quarter inches long; and two round headed brass screws. Bend the wider brass strip around the brass rod to form a slider. Bend the narrow brass strip in the center to form a V spring. Solder one end of this to the slider so that it is in the position shown in the drawing. Slip the slider on the brass rod, place the rod in position directly over the pathway of bared wire on the coil so that the lower end of the V spring will press on this pathway, and fasten the rod securely with the brass screws to the wooden end pieces.

For the "aërial" get three or four hundred feet of wire—No. 16 galvanized wire will do, though aluminum or copper wire is better—some insulator knobs, and two cross spreaders three feet long. The parallel wires in the aërial should be at least two feet apart, and the aërial should be placed as high as possible so that surrounding buildings, etc., will not interfere with the wireless wave. The bare wires, wherever they are fastened to poles or trees must, of course, be wound around insulators. For a ground connection, fasten an ordinary insulated wire to a water pipe or to a piece of iron pipe sunk five feet in damp ground. A safety switch may be made, like the drawing, from a piece of wood six inches square and an inch thick, a piece of stiff brass three inches long and a half inch wide, and three round-headed brass screws.

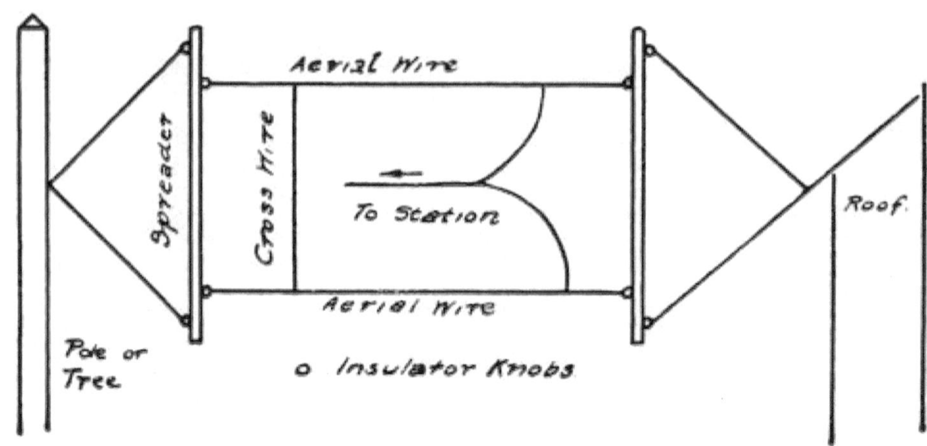

Aerial.

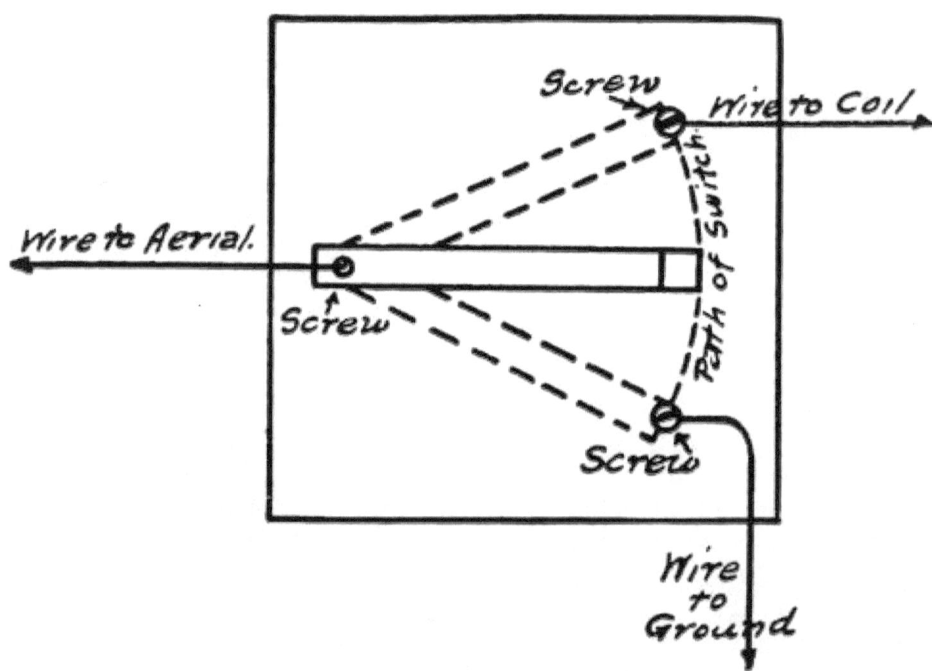

Switch.

This completes the separate parts of the receiving apparatus. To connect it up for use, follow the circuit diagram. One wire from the aërial leads through the safety switch to the tuning coil. From the tuning coil carry an insulated wire to the detector, and from the detector to the ground. The receiver has two wires leading from it—one to a point between the detector and the tuning coil, and the other to a similar point between the detector and the ground. When not in use the aërial should be connected directly with the ground by means of the safety switch. Where two wires are connected they must of course have the insulation scraped off so that bare wire rests against bare wire.

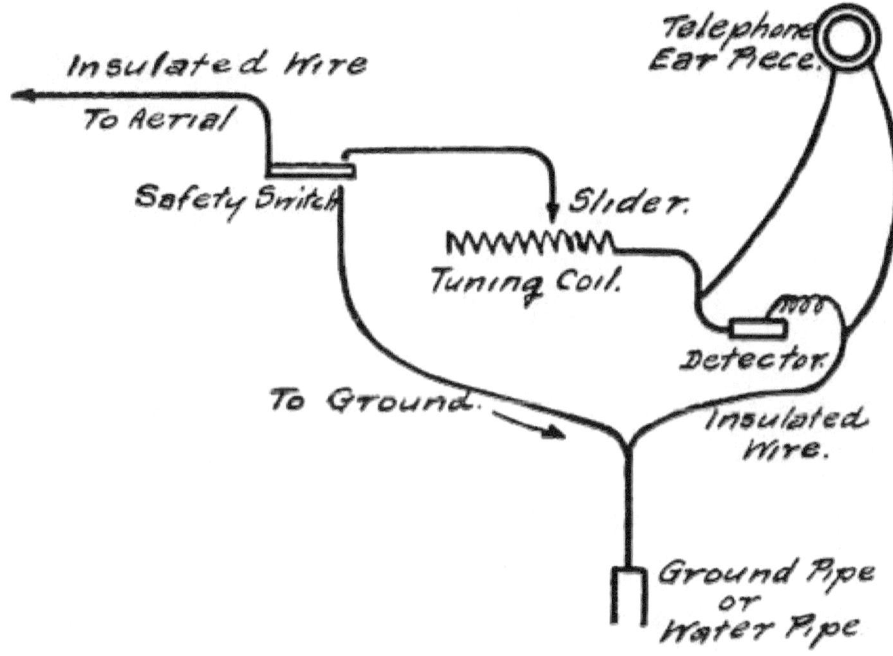

Diagram of Circuit.

When you have learned to translate your messages you will be able to do quite a bit of wireless eavesdropping, and your receiver will click with countless messages.

THE END.

Lector House believes that a society develops through a two-fold approach of continuous learning and adaptation, which is derived from the study of classic literary works spread across the historic timeline of literature records. Therefore, we aim at reviving, repairing and redeveloping all those inaccessible or damaged but historically as well as culturally important literature across subjects so that the future generations may have an opportunity to study and learn from past works to embark upon a journey of creating a better future.

This book is a result of an effort made by Lector House towards making a contribution to the preservation and repair of original ancient works which might hold historical significance to the approach of continuous learning across subjects.

HAPPY READING & LEARNING!

LECTOR HOUSE LLP
E-MAIL: lectorpublishing@gmail.com